Mastering AI Governance: A Guide to Building Trustworthy and Transparent AI Systems

Dinesh Rajshekharan

notionpress.com

INDIA • SINGAPORE • MALAYSIA

ISBN
Paperback 9798905104800
Hardcase 9798905104817

Dedication

To my family, for their love, patience, and quiet strength.

For the teachers, mentors, colleagues, and friends who shaped the way I think about technology, responsibility, and human values.

And for everyone working to ensure that the future of artificial intelligence remains grounded in trust, wisdom, and service to humanity.

Contents

Forward

While AI might be humanity's greatest opportunity, simultaneously it is potentially one of our greatest disasters. And humans have a predictable way to react to both!

First comes denial. We convince ourselves the change is overhyped, temporary, or someone else's problem. Organizations may abdicate their obligation to govern AI, deploying AI systems without fully understanding their risks, their biases, or the consequences of automated decision-making at scale. This book confronts that denial directly by emphasizing transparency, accountability, fairness, risk management, and continuous oversight as foundational requirements for trustworthy AI systems.

The second stage of every crisis is searching for reassurance from others. We ask our friends, colleagues, peers, family, and even religious or political leaders. "Are you worried about about this thing? What do you think?" In AI governance, this instinct has produced frameworks, principles, and policies across nations and industries. Yet frameworks alone are insufficient. The challenge is no longer merely defining ethical principles—it is operationalizing them in real time.

That is where decisive action becomes the dividing line between resilient organizations and vulnerable ones. Some enterprises freeze, overwhelmed by the complexity of AI, uncertain where accountability begins or ends. Others move toward a new operational model: governance as a continuous, measurable, and provable discipline. In many ways, this aligns with the emerging concept of GovOps—the evolution of governance from static oversight into an operational control plane. GovOps recognizes that trust cannot depend solely on policies written by humans; it must also be enforced through analyzable policy, verifiable identity, runtime telemetry, and continuous evidence generation.

This book provides the foundations for that transformation. It explains why transparency, stakeholder accountability, risk assessment, incident response, and ethical AI are not isolated activities, but interconnected operational capabilities. The future of AI governance will belong to organizations that can move beyond compliance theater toward systems that continuously prove their integrity, resilience, and trustworthiness under real-world conditions.

In the end, AI governance is not about controlling machines—it is about proving humans still control the consequences. Governance is no longer the brake on innovation—it is the steering wheel.

– Mike Schwartz

Founder and CEO of Gluu

Preface

Artificial intelligence has moved from research labs and technical experiments into the operating core of modern society. It now shapes decisions about hiring, lending, healthcare, education, public services, cybersecurity, and the everyday experiences of millions of people. As AI systems become more capable, more autonomous, and more deeply embedded in institutions, the question before us is no longer whether AI should be governed. The real question is how to govern it well.

This book was written in response to that question.

AI governance is often misunderstood as a narrow compliance exercise or as a set of abstract ethical aspirations. In practice, it is neither. Governance is the discipline that connects values to execution. It is the mechanism by which organizations translate principles such as fairness, accountability, transparency, privacy, safety, and human oversight into real operating systems: policies, controls, reviews, audits, documentation, incident response, and decision rights. Without governance, even well-intentioned AI programs can drift into inconsistency, opacity, regulatory exposure, or harm. With governance, organizations have a path to build trust while still enabling innovation.

The purpose of this book is to provide that path in a clear and practical way.

Across these chapters, I have tried to approach AI governance as both a strategic necessity and an operational capability. The book begins by grounding the reader in the foundations of AI governance: what it is, why it matters, how regulation and policy have evolved, and which stakeholders shape the governance landscape. It then moves into the attributes of trustworthy AI, including fairness, privacy, accountability, and risk mitigation. From there, the discussion turns to transparency and explainability, because no system that materially affects people can remain a black box forever. The later chapters focus on regulation, legal obligations, cross-border data challenges, governance structures, monitoring, incident response, and the work of sustaining governance over time.

My hope is that readers will see governance not as friction, but as architecture. Good governance does not slow serious innovation; it makes serious innovation possible. It creates the confidence to scale. It helps organizations ask better questions before deployment, respond better when systems fail, and learn faster as technology and regulation evolve. In that sense, governance is not the opposite of progress. It is what makes progress durable.

This book is intended for a wide audience: students seeking a structured introduction to responsible AI, practitioners building or deploying AI systems, product and engineering leaders designing organizational controls, policymakers and compliance professionals interpreting regulatory change, and executives who need to understand both the promise and the risk of AI-enabled transformation. Some readers may come to this subject from law, some from technology, some from ethics, and some from business. I have written with all of them in mind.

The field itself is evolving rapidly. New model architectures, new use cases, new standards, and new laws continue to reshape what responsible AI requires in practice. Because of that, no single book can offer a final word on AI governance. What it can offer is a framework for thinking, a vocabulary for collaboration, and a practical foundation for action. If this book helps readers move from vague concern to disciplined governance, from reactive control to intentional design, or from fragmented efforts to a more coherent strategy, it will have served its purpose.

Ultimately, AI governance is about preserving human agency in a world of increasingly intelligent systems. It is about ensuring that the technologies we build remain aligned with the values we claim to hold. It is about trust, not as a slogan, but as a system. And it is about recognizing that the future of AI will be shaped not only by what these systems can do, but by the care with which we choose to govern them.

I invite you to read this book with both curiosity and responsibility: curiosity about what AI can enable, and responsibility for the standards that must guide its development and use. The future of AI will not be determined by capability alone. It will also be determined by governance.

Acknowledgements

This book was made possible through the support, encouragement, and inspiration of many people.

I am deeply grateful to my family for their patience, understanding, and unwavering support throughout the writing process. Their belief in me created the space and strength needed to bring this work to life.

I would also like to thank the many colleagues, mentors, leaders, and teams I have worked with over the years across security, identity, privacy, platform engineering, and governance. My professional journey has given me the opportunity to engage with complex questions at the intersection of technology, responsibility, and trust. Those experiences have shaped much of the thinking reflected in these pages.

I am grateful to the broader community of researchers, policymakers, practitioners, and educators whose work continues to advance the field of AI governance. Their contributions have helped build a much-needed foundation for more transparent, accountable, and human-centered AI systems.

Finally, I would like to thank every reader who chooses to engage seriously with this subject. AI governance is not only a technical or regulatory challenge; it is a human one. I hope this book contributes, in some small way, to building systems that are worthy of trust and aligned with the values we want to carry forward.

Chapter 1

Foundations of AI Governance

1.1 Understanding AI Governance: Concepts and Importance

AI governance refers to a system or framework that guarantees that an AI application is ethical. This includes all the legal or regulatory frameworks that inform the application of AI, with the aim of ensuring accountability, transparency, and compliance with AI principles (Fitz-Gerald, Ganesh, Nathwani, Niazi, & Herdem, 2026).

How does AI Governance operate to ensure ethics?

To guarantee the use of AI ethically and within the regulations, AI Governance develops a framework and norms. It contains the following aspects:

1. **Ethical Standards:** The document establishes the objectives that AI system development and deployment processes must achieve to establish fair and responsible systems that operate with transparent functions.

2. **Developing Policies:** This part of the process includes making rules to control how AI is used, to deal with potential dangers, and to encourage ethical innovation.

3. **Ensuring Compliance:** Establishes mechanisms to monitor compliance with rules and regulations, guaranteeing that organizations fulfill their ethical and legal responsibilities.

4. **Engagement of stakeholders:** Facilitates collaborations among lawmakers, tech firms, and ordinary people to ensure that the policies concerning AI are in alignment with social ideals.

5. **Best practices:** Sets out requirements that firms need to meet, such as conducting audits on a regular basis, carrying out impact assessments, and offering training to their employees.

6. **Risk Management:** Identifies potential risks associated with AI systems and ways in which they can be addressed.

Together, these elements make up a powerful model for governing AI systems, thereby promoting AI ethics and boosting public trust.

Common Uses and Applications of AI Governance

Governance plays a vital role in different fields to help achieve responsible AI. Here are some areas of AI governance application:

1. **Regulatory Compliance:** In order to ensure that AI technologies are developed in accordance with legal regulations, AI governance frameworks are implemented to meet both domestic and international legislation.

2. **Ethical AI Development:** Businesses develop strategies to promote the ethical development of AI systems, focusing on transparency, accountability, and fairness.

3. **Risk Mitigation:** AI governance helps identify and manage risks associated with the introduction of AI technologies, including risks of bias or unethical development of AI models.

4. **Stakeholder Engagement:** Effective AI governance involves stakeholder engagement as it promotes trust between companies and consumers or civil societies in AI development.

5. **Monitoring System Performance:** Organizations use governance frameworks to regularly review the system performance and avoid possible harms that AI technologies might bring.

6. **Data Management:** In order to address the issue of data protection; AI governance framework often relies on best practices of data stewardship.

7. **Training and Awareness:** An essential part of the implementation process involves training of employees on governance issues and the importance of ethical AI technologies.

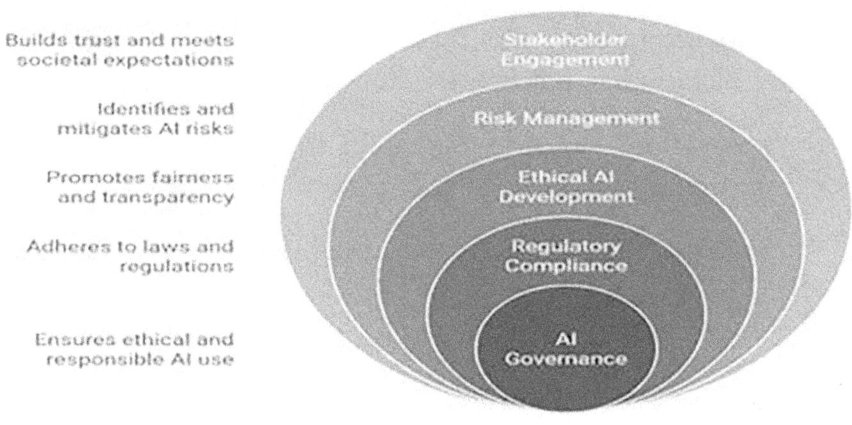

Figure 1.1: AI Governance Framework

Source: (Team, 2024)

What are the advantages of AI Governance?

AI Governance is essential for ensuring the proper use of artificial intelligence. Some of the advantages that can be derived from proper governance include:

1. **Ethics Compliance:** Guarantees that any technology used will be done so within proper ethical boundaries.
2. **Government Compliance:** Assists companies in ensuring they adhere to all existing AI policies and regulations.
3. **Trust Building:** Helps to establish trust among stakeholders because of ethical AI management.
4. **Risk Management:** Helps an organization to identify and manage risks related to its AI technology.
5. **Implementation of Best Practices:** Helps organizations implement best practices regarding the AI technology.
6. **Innovation:** Supports innovation and ethical standards at the same time.
7. **Sustainability:** Helps an organization ensure that its AI technology is sustainable.

What are the Expected Future Trends for AI Governance?

The anticipated modifications in AI regulation would entail the implementation of adaptive regulatory frameworks, collaboration among international organizations, and technological means to enforce compliance. The increased trust and improved ethics related to AI systems would be realized through these anticipated modifications.

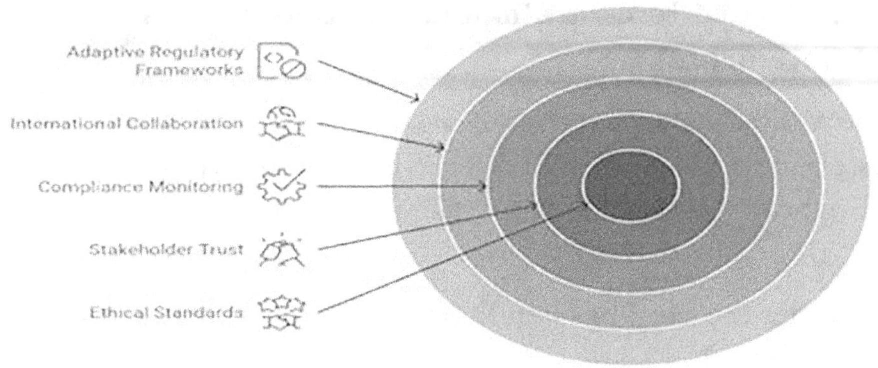

Figure 1.2: Future of AI Governance

Source: (Team, 2024)

What are the Best Practices for Using AI Governance Effectively?

AI Governance may be employed effectively by:

1. Formulating specific policies to provide guidelines on the ethical use of AI.
2. Conducting stakeholder engagement sessions.
3. Monitoring AI usage to ensure compliance.
4. Educating teams on ethical usage of AI.

Are there Detailed Case Studies Demonstrating the Successful Implementation of AI Governance?

A governance tool can be seen through the example of IBM. In its artificial intelligence software development, IBM has made use of the agent model, which focuses heavily on transparency and accountability. Thus, IBM was able to improve its reputation score due to the increased confidence of its stakeholders and adherence to global laws.

What Related Terms are Important to Understand along with AI Governance?

The AI Ethics and Compliance Framework are related concepts that lay the groundwork for ethical AI development and deployment; as such, they are essential to comprehending AI Governance.

What are the Step-by-Step Instructions for Implementing AI Governance?

To ensure effective AI Governance, organizations should adopt the following best practices:

The following best practices can facilitate effective AI Governance:

1. **Develop Ethical Standards:** The need for an ethical standards regime for AI governance cannot be overemphasized. A clear outline of the ethical standards expected while developing and utilizing AI will ensure compliance.

2. **Involve Stakeholders in AI Governance:** Different stakeholders like policymakers, technologists, legal experts, and citizens at large should be involved in formulating the AI governance framework to enhance its relevance to society.

3. **Monitor the Compliance Status of AI Systems:** AI systems should be constantly monitored for adherence to the set governance framework. Constant monitoring facilitates the discovery of any risk to the organization.

4. **Secure the Data:** Securing data used in the development and application of AI systems is vital for protecting the confidentiality and integrity of the information.

5. **Conduct Impact Assessments:** Conduct impact assessment on the use of AI to identify ethical, bias, and other risks involved before the implementation of the AI project.

6. **Conduct Awareness Campaigns:** To facilitate the implementation of AI Governance policies and practices, organizations should conduct awareness campaigns to educate stakeholders.
7. **Adapting to Regulatory Changes:** Keep track of regulatory changes and make sure your governance models can adapt to any change in laws and ethics, thus avoiding any legal issues and remaining consistent with international norms.
8. **Enhancing Transparency:** Be completely transparent about the way your AI works, the input data, and the methods used for decision-making. This will establish more trust between AI systems and end users.
9. **Having a Crisis Management Plan:** Should anything go wrong with the AI system, you should be prepared to deal with the problem promptly and transparently. Develop an action plan to follow in cases of ethical violations or malfunctions.
10. **Cultivating an Organizational Culture of Accountability:** Establish a culture of accountability in which each stakeholder in the process of AI system design and implementation knows their responsibility in the matter.

Why Is AI Governance Important?

The field of generative AI is still in its infancy, and when AI produces inconsistent results, many businesses encounter difficulties. They may suffer financial losses, damage to their reputation, and regulatory attention as a result. In the end, companies run the risk of lagging behind rivals and possibly making headlines as a result of insufficient AI regulation if they don't have effective control over AI and its data. To avoid problems like bias, unjust decision-making, and human rights breaches in AI systems, it is essential to develop fundamental rules for AI ethics.

For example, remote tutoring company iTutor Group had to pay $365,000[1] to settle a suit[2] for unlawful age discrimination. It used an AI-powered recruiting software that automatically rejected female applicants ages 55 and older and male applicants ages 60 and older. Similarly, Air Canada was ordered to pay damages to a passenger after its virtual assistant gave him incorrect information related to availing of a bereavement discount.[3]

Below are some ways that highlight the importance of AI governance for modern enterprises:

- **Loss of Trust** – AI governance aids in upholding norms for the ethical and responsible application of AI. Without enough supervision, AI systems may act erratically, producing results that users cannot comprehend or rely on.
- **Increased Risk** – The operations and activities of businesses might be disrupted by ungoverned AI solutions. Without measures to protect the ethical use of data and AI, an organization becomes vulnerable to cyber risks and vulnerabilities.
- **Resisting the Use of AI Solutions** – Resistance is another possible effect associated with the lack of AI governance. People tend to resist change, especially in cases where people do not understand something. Lack of AI governance means employees and other stakeholders might lack confidence in the capabilities of AI.
- **Inconsistent Results** – AI solutions without governance tend to provide inconsistent results. AI algorithms may hallucinate and deliver misleading insights owing to poor-quality, imbalanced, and erroneous datasets. Such an outcome can undermine operations and decision-making processes.
- **Non-Compliance with Regulations** – There is a need to comply with all the AI rules and policies. AI solutions may accidentally violate various AI regulations, including those regarding discrimination or privacy, without defined guidelines.

- **Bad Reputation of Brands** – Ungoverned AI solutions may provide misleading insights, make poor business decisions, and face various kinds of security breaches. The negative publicity associated with such issues might damage the reputation and image of brands.

What Are the Business Benefits of AI Governance?

AI holds great promise; however, without proper and ethical regulation, it might lead to issues such as moral dilemmas and misuse of AI. The governance of AI helps organizations leverage the benefits of AI and manage risks in a variety of ways:

- **Enhance AI results reliability:** The increased reliability of AI results is attained through governance of artificial intelligence, which helps create frameworks that ensure accountability, transparency, and quality assurance. Governance directs the development and utilization of the AI system, making it possible to rely on accurate, objective and superior-quality data.

- **Limit the likelihood of non-compliance:** Organizational compliance to the set rules can be easily demonstrated and non-compliance resolved with ease when norms and standards are set. Non-compliance will result in costly fines and penalties, which can be avoided by adopting an AI governance approach.

- **AI Explainability:** With a transparent AI system, the organization can understand and communicate how the AI-driven decisions are generated. Understanding of the process makes it easier for the organization to make better decisions, improve efficiency, and realize strategic objectives.

- **Secure collaboration:** AI governance introduces guidelines for data and AI usage within the firm. Innovation is encouraged, and access to data is protected through the implementation of safeguards to secure access to AI and data. Collaboration is fostered in a safe manner to mitigate any risk associated with AI.

- **Build stakeholder trust:** AI governance addresses the problems associated with implementing AI through creating a predictable and dependable system. AI governance eliminates the problem of distrust in the application of AI since it offers visibility into how AI works by highlighting the steps involved in generating dependable and reliable data. Issues of accuracy, fairness, regulatory compliance, and use also get addressed through AI governance, which promotes trust. This helps facilitate scale.
- **Facilitate AI literacy:** AI governance enables the formulation and implementation of standard and understandable procedures regarding the use of AI. This allows for greater access to AI and understanding of AI concepts both for experts and non-experts. Training also gets supported through AI governance since it helps to educate employees about AI concepts.

1.2 The Evolution of AI Regulation and Policy

AI regulations provide the boundaries of the growth, usage, and impact of such systems on individuals. Strong principles can be used to make tech equitable and secure - no damage to the community or civic confidence. These include the risks of security, ethical issues, and protection and storage of personal information. The system does not disregard the risks, mainly when decisions go wrong. And we cannot afford to wait before the issues become widespread.

AI is making assertive steps - morals, laws, and daily life are being consumed Privacy is being cannibalized. Workers can be substituted with machines. Cyberattacks grow smarter. There is a fear that AI will eliminate human supremacy. We cannot discount the motivation it has on the transformation of lives - just look at the results. Regulations are significant yet practical effect is too.

Without the right regulations, AI may be misused or abused and the consequences may be very detrimental. As an example, the AI can be used to propagate propaganda or misinformation, which can cause severe social issues. On another dimension, it can be employed to infringe the privacy of people or carry out cyberattacks. On the one hand, an AI that is free of limitations is a threat to human life.

Should AI Be Regulated?

The issue of AI regulation exists as a topic that people can debate. The first argument states that all technological production and consumption need regulation to ensure ethical practices during use and to prevent technological abuse. The other people believe that excessive regulations will prevent companies from innovating new products while they will also impede the growth of artificial intelligence businesses.

Among the major tech companies, such as OpenAI, Google, and Microsoft, there is a growing consensus that regulation is needed. It must, however, be designed thoughtfully to keep up with the current development of AI technology and take into consideration the dynamic and unpredictable nature of the field.

Regulation will be able to provide a guideline of how AI should be responsibly used, ensuring that it is used in a manner that is fair, ethical, and will not harm society. Also, it may provide defense against potential abuse of the technology. The regulation should not be excessively restrictive, however, since this may curb the social and economic benefits of AI developments.

Key Parameters Shaping Regulations and Their Outcomes

Transparency, Fairness, and Explainability

The principles of transparency, fairness, and explainability are fundamental to ensuring that AI is used responsibly and ethically:

- **Transparency:** This is the ability to understand how an AI system makes decisions. This is essential since it allows individuals to understand the logic behind the decision of a system and may help build technological trust.

- **Fairness:** Fairness is an important element, and it entails fairness where AI systems do not favor specific groups or individuals. This would be crucial in making sure that the benefits of AI are shared equally across the society and in ensuring that AI is not abused to serve an evil purpose.
- **Explain ability:** In the ability to explain the working of an AI system is capacity explained. This plays a vital role in making sure that individuals understand the process of decision-making and in building trust in the technology.

Risk-Based Approach

The risk-based approach to AI regulation requires organizations to assess all potential dangers linked to AI systems before they start creating regulations for danger mitigation. The regulatory system developed through this method enables continuous development because it can adapt to both changing technological needs and upcoming AI advancements.

The risk-based approach involves:

- Identifying potential risks
- Assessing their likelihood and potential impact
- Identifying how risks could manifest across different types of AI technology
- Developing strategies to manage these risks in specific contexts

Addressing Security Risks and Malicious Actors

Security considerations within AI procedures focus on the misuse and potential use of the AI technology to perform cyberattacks, whereas risk-based talks largely ensure the assessment of the potential risks from AI.

Security risks are multifaceted and involve safeguarding AI technologies, adhering to ethical standards, and developing mechanisms for accountability and compensation.

The worst offenders who employ AI in their crimes may be brought to task only when there are effective means available to combat cybercrime, in conjunction with collaboration between government agencies, businesses, and cybersecurity professionals.

Institutional Approach

One of the components of the institutional approach to AI regulation is the establishment of special organizations or agencies that regulate AI development and use. These bodies would ensure the law is enforced, compliance is monitored and any arising disputes or problems.

An institutional approach can be used to regulate AI in a more coordinated and comprehensive way and, therefore, may offer a more powerful and effective regulatory framework. It may also be used as a platform of dialogue and cooperation between different stakeholders, such as government, industry, academia and civil society.

International Harmonization

International harmonization is the method by which several countries or areas arrive at a common set of AI rules. The mechanism stops firms from relocating to jurisdictions with more lenient regulations and, at the same time, creates a level playing field for AI development and usage. Through the process of international harmonization, countries can handle the advantages and downsides of AI, while at the same time, they open up avenues for global partnerships and collaborations. But, since political, legal, and cultural systems vary, achieving international harmonization may be a challenge.

With AI technologies becoming more and more common, the desire for international harmonization is also increasing. Since AI systems are developed and used globally, a coordinated global approach is needed to handle the pros and cons of this technology.

History of AI Regulations and Laws Around the World

1. **United States of America**

   In fact, there is currently no widely imposed federal law at all that regulates AI usage in the US. In October 2022, the Biden administration revealed an AI Bill of Rights that covered areas such as safety and efficacy, protection from discrimination by algorithms, transparency and explanation, data privacy, and availability of human alternatives and fallback. US lawmakers introduced the National AI Panel Act in June 2023, which would create a government panel responsible for reviewing the nation's AI policy approach.

   In October 2023, the White House revealed the AI Executive Order (EO 14110) at the same time. It lays out a structure for the design, execution, and oversight of artificial intelligence (AI) technology in government agencies and will be extended nationwide. The paper aims to promote AI innovation but still ensure that AI development is ethical, safe, and protective of civil rights and privacy.

2. **United Kingdom**

   UK has taken the lead in creating a regulatory framework that fosters the ethical progress of AI technologies. The UK's AI strategy rests on the idea of leveraging the country's excellence in innovation, ethics and governance. A big step was the creation of the Center for Data Ethics and Innovation (CDEI), a body that counsels the government on matters of AI and data governance.

CDEI drafts frameworks and assists in laying down rules to regulate the use of AI technologies appropriately. Besides, the UK's AI strategy mentions public sector innovation, setting ethical standards, and having a skilled workforce as the three main pillars through which the UK can sustain its leadership in the AI field.

3. **EU**

The AI Act that has been proposed by the EU demonstrates its commitment to the development of AI in an ethical manner. The initiative is seen as pioneering legislation when it comes to setting out comprehensive AI regulations. This law seeks to establish fair guidelines that ensure that the rights of citizens are protected while ensuring competitiveness. The regulations also seek to classify AI technology according to its level of risk and impose stringent rules on high-risk applications such as employment, education, and policing.

Regulation of AI that emphasizes accountability, transparency, and data governance has created a standard for regulatory approaches worldwide. The formation of an AI board in Europe is a direct indication of the Union's effort to harmonize AI laws in the member countries. Consequently, the EU guarantees an effective approach toward AI governance.

4. **Japan**

The Japanese AI policy highlights the need for the incorporation of AI technology within their economy and society, focusing on innovation, security, and ethical concerns. The Japanese government has taken initiatives to improve the country's competitive advantage in the global AI industry through the funding of AI R&D programs.

Japan seeks to accelerate the implementation of AI in diverse sectors like health care, manufacturing, and transport by encouraging an environment that encourages collaboration among business, academic institutions, and the government. To ensure proper usage of AI technology, Japan is creating guidelines related to ethical AI with a focus on security, transparency, and privacy.

5. **Australia**

   It is clear that the Australian approach to the regulation of artificial intelligence would help foster innovation and make sure that any innovation is done ethically. It must be said that the Australian government has developed an AI strategy that proves its readiness to become a leader in the development and application of this technology.

   In order to ensure that AI deployment would benefit society and the country's economy, Australians try to build trust among citizens towards AI by fostering transparency and inclusiveness.

6. **Canada**

   At present, Canada is endeavoring to establish guidelines that will help in the ethical development and deployment of AI technology, for which it is known for its notable contributions to researching AI technology. The Canadian government has devised plans to make Canada a frontrunner in terms of AI technology innovation.

   The plans highlight the importance of developing ethical AI, conducting world-class research, and using AI technology to drive economic growth. As part of its strategy to ensure that AI is used for the benefit of society and the economy, Canada's strategy encompasses initiatives to train an AI workforce and foster partnerships between the government, academia, and industry.

7. **Brazil**

   Given the possibilities offered by AI technology in terms of innovation, Brazil is beginning to harness AI technology to drive innovation for its economy and society. There have been discussions related to AI technology by the Brazilian government, focusing particularly on developing workers' AI skills, innovation, and ethics.

   The government wishes to deploy AI technology to help solve various challenges within the country, such as issues regarding the environment, healthcare, and education. With regard to adhering to the same international standards in creating and implementing AI technologies, the government has also taken into account international cooperation.

8. **China**

   As far as the Chinese strategy regarding AI goes, China has invested heavily into researching and developing AI with the aim of achieving world dominance of AI technologies by 2030. The Chinese government seeks to ensure that the power of AI to drive technological and economic progress does not compromise the social stability of the country; therefore, state coordination is an important feature of the Chinese regulations concerning AI.

   As part of their AI strategy, the Chinese have laws that encourage collaboration among the government, industry, and academia when it comes to creating new AI innovations. China states that they are focusing on establishing the ethical framework of AI in order to deal with security, privacy, and equality issues.

Evolution of AI Policy

The history of the policy surrounding AI is a testimony to how powerful an impact intelligent systems have made and continue to make on different aspects of life, ranging from society and the economy to governance and international security. With the continued development of AI from mere theories to tangible applications, lawmakers across the globe have had to continuously update their regulations to account for any ramifications.

1. **Early Foundations of AI Policy (Pre-2000s)**

   In the early stages of AI development, policy considerations were minimal. AI was largely confined to academic research and experimental applications.

   Key Characteristics:

   Limited government involvement in AI regulation

   Focus on research funding rather than governance

   Ethical discussions primarily theoretical

   Important Points:

   AI research was supported by governments through defense and academic grants

   Concerns about automation and job displacement began to emerge

   Ethical considerations were influenced by philosophical debates rather than practical issues

2. **Emergence of Digital Policy Frameworks (2000–2010)**

   With the rapid growth of the internet and digital technologies, early policy frameworks began to take shape.

   Key Characteristics:

   Rise of data protection and privacy laws

   Initial discussions on algorithmic accountability

   Recognition of AI's economic potential

Important Points:

Governments introduced data protection laws to regulate digital information

Early frameworks focused on cybersecurity and information governance

AI began to be recognized as a strategic sector for economic growth

Limited but growing awareness of bias in automated systems

3. **Expansion of AI Governance (2010–2016)**

This period marked a turning point as AI technologies, particularly machine learning, became more powerful and widely adopted.

Key Characteristics:

Increased global interest in AI policy

Emergence of ethical AI principles

Government-led AI strategies

Important Points:

Countries began launching national AI strategies

Ethical concerns such as bias, transparency, and accountability gained attention

Big data and machine learning raised privacy challenges

Tech companies started playing a major role in shaping AI governance

4. **Formalization of AI Policies and Guidelines (2016–2020)**

During this phase, AI policy became more structured and formalized across nations and international organizations.

Key Characteristics:

Development of ethical AI guidelines

Increased regulatory efforts

International collaboration

Important Points:

Governments introduced AI-specific policy frameworks

Ethical principles such as fairness, transparency, and accountability became central

International organizations promoted responsible AI use

Public awareness about AI risks increased significantly

Regulatory discussions on autonomous systems (e.g., self-driving cars) intensified

5. **Regulatory Acceleration and Global Competition (2020–Present)**

AI policy has entered a phase of rapid development, driven by technological breakthroughs and geopolitical competition.

Key Characteristics:

Stronger regulatory frameworks

Emphasis on trustworthy and human-centric AI

AI as a strategic geopolitical asset

Important Points:

Governments are introducing stricter AI regulations and compliance requirements

Focus on ethical AI, human rights, and safety

Increased scrutiny of big tech companies

AI governance linked to national security and global competitiveness

Development of standards for AI safety, transparency, and accountability

Rise of AI auditing and impact assessments

Challenges in AI Policy Development

Despite progress, several challenges persist in creating effective AI policies:

Important Points:

Rapid technological change outpacing regulation

Difficulty in defining and standardizing AI systems

Balancing innovation with regulation

Lack of global consensus on AI governance

Enforcement and compliance issues

Ethical dilemmas in real-world implementation

Role of International Cooperation

AI policy is increasingly shaped by global collaboration among governments, organizations, and institutions.

Important Points:

Development of international AI standards

Cross-border data sharing agreements

Collaborative research initiatives

Global discussions on AI ethics and safety

Efforts to prevent misuse of AI technologies

1.3 Key Stakeholders in AI Governance

GenAI has the ability to transform several industries, such as the health industry, financial industry, education industry, and others. The development and implementation of genAI involve a governance model because of its ability to generate content, detect patterns, and simulate human interaction. The role and responsibilities of key stakeholders play a significant part in ensuring regulation, maintaining moral values, and managing the impact of GenAI on society.

There are several key parties participating in the process of GenAI regulation. These are mainly governments and respective regulatory bodies. Their responsibility is the development and implementation of the legislation that will ensure the moral use of AI technologies. The governments should find a balance between innovations, people's safety, and ethics. There is a good example that can be given in terms of GDPR (General Data Protection Regulation) issued in the EU. It is clear that GDPR has created an example of strict data protection regulation concerning AI technologies and their application. Such restrictive measures are needed in order to avoid any potential misuse of AI and to make sure that people's rights are respected in the course of using AI technologies. The problem is that it is difficult for the government to keep pace with technology development and to create proper regulations.

Through their research and contributions to knowledge, educational institutions provide an important contribution to the governance of GenAI. Such organizations are at the cutting edge of technology, understanding the opportunities and limitations of AI technologies. They help in assessing the risks and ethical challenges associated with GenAI through conducting independent research. Additionally, they educate future AI practitioners about the importance of ethical considerations in AI by stressing the importance of ethical considerations in AI design and implementation. For example, the Partnership on AI is made up of non-profit organizations, commercial enterprises, and universities aiming at researching and developing good practice in AI technologies. Such partnerships result in research findings that inform legislation and policy-making regarding ethical considerations in AI use.

Businesses and industrial leaders are key stakeholders who significantly contribute to the implementation of GenAI governance. Being involved in developing and using such technologies, they become essential participants in the creation of AI technology design. The big corporations investing millions of dollars into AI development like Google, OpenAI, and IBM, make an immense contribution to the progress of the whole industry. However, great power entails great responsibility. These companies should be sure that they create accessible and ethical AI technologies. Corporate governance frameworks that put ethical considerations at the forefront can serve as an exemplary standard. For instance, Google's guidelines for developing AI have been used as a benchmark by prioritizing fairness, transparency, and privacy. The application of such considerations by businesses allows for mitigating the risks associated with GenAI technologies.

The importance of incorporating the interests of the public in GenAI governance requires civil society organizations such as NGOs. They act as a watchdog for both corporate and government actors in the development and deployment of AI technologies. They ensure that the actions of companies and governments are accountable and that there is no violation of human rights by the technology or perpetuation of discrimination. For example, the Algorithmic Justice League seeks to promote socially responsible use of AI technology. Through civil society, the development of a more responsible AI governance structure can be achieved through problem-solving, such as bias and discrimination by algorithms.

The participation of international organizations is equally important in the governance of GenAI. Since the problems involved in this regard, such as privacy, security, and ethics, can be transnational, it is necessary to cooperate internationally. AI can be regulated by developing worldwide regulations and standards in partnership with organizations such as the United Nations and the Organization for Economic Cooperation and

Development (OECD). One example is the OECD AI Principles, which are human-centered and emphasize fairness and serve as guidelines for the responsible use of AI.

Inclusion of the perspectives of all stakeholders in the governance model of GenAI makes the model more effective. Collaboration between various stakeholders is crucial in order to address the challenging issues caused by the development of artificial intelligence technology. The collaboration between different governmental bodies, research institutions, businesses, and other social institutions guarantees that the development and application of GenAI take into account ethical and societal considerations.

In conclusion, there should be numerous stakeholders participating in the governance of GenAI due to its collaborative nature. The role of legislation is to ensure the application of GenAI technology in an ethical and safe manner with the help of government institutions and other regulating bodies. The academic community provides data on the capabilities and constraints of AI technology. Business leaders promote innovation alongside ethics. In the public interest, civil society organizations promote accountability and openness. International organizations support the creation of international norms and international collaboration. These parties work together to create a strong governance structure that guarantees the ethical development and application of GenAI. These stakeholders' cooperation and dedication will be crucial to maximizing GenAI's potential while preserving moral standards and social ideals as AI technologies advance.

Why Identify Key Stakeholders?

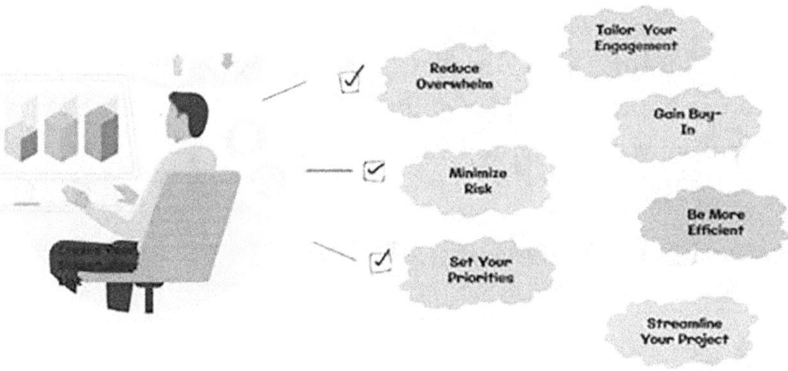

Figure 1.3: Key Stakeholders

Source: (Hendricks, 2024)

There are a number of reasons project managers or consultation teams will usually identify key stakeholders as part of their engagement or consultation process. Identifying key stakeholders can help with:

- **Reducing Overwhelm** – Go from an overwhelming list of hundreds of potential stakeholders to a more manageable list that you can realistically engage with.
- **Minimizing Risk** – Identify which stakeholders present a higher potential risk and engage with them early on in the project.
- **Setting Priorities** – Take a more strategic approach to your engagement by prioritizing communications and engagement activities where you can have the greatest impact.
- **Tailoring Your Engagement** – Key stakeholders will likely need to get more frequent and/or detailed updates.
- **Gaining Buy-In** – Get buy-in from the stakeholders who will have the biggest impact on your project.

- **Being More Efficient** – Focus your time and resources where they matter most, and efficiently engage with a smaller list of key stakeholders.
- **Streamline Your Project** – By engaging frequently with key stakeholders who play an important role in your project, you can ensure your operations run smoothly.

Steps to Identify Key Stakeholders

Figure 1.4: Steps to Identify Key Stakeholders

Source: (Hendricks, 2024)

There are four main steps to figuring out who your key stakeholders are, and then using these insights in your project or consultation.

Step 1: Creating Your Stakeholder List

The process of stakeholder identification begins with a foundational step: developing a comprehensive stakeholder list. In order to effectively engage and prioritize, it is important to first get a clear idea of who the stakeholders are. This is an important step that requires some amount of planning because the success of the analysis depends on how accurate the stakeholder identification has been.

To begin with, all individuals who might have an interest in the project or be affected by the initiative should be identified. This will include internal parties like the workers, managers, executives, and external parties, including clients, suppliers, government authorities, and many more. It is important to note that the primary focus of this step is to identify all the potential stakeholders.

Brainstorming is seen to be very useful in achieving this goal. Using brainstorming techniques, both structured and unstructured, it is possible for many ideas regarding stakeholder identification to be generated. It is very important to think outside the box since there might be stakeholders who are indirectly affected by this activity. Cooperation is definitely useful in this case because using other people's ideas will help you realize some other options as well.

Apart from brainstorming, there are other techniques that could facilitate the process of identifying stakeholders. Geographic techniques and mapping systems can assist in locating people and organizations located in the immediate vicinity of the project being undertaken. Likewise, techniques that involve engaging with the community, such as outreach programs and questionnaires, can shed light on the identity of those stakeholders impacted by the project.

As for the creation of the stakeholders' list, there comes another challenge when the number of stakeholders exceeds the company's capabilities of interacting with them on an individual basis. This is quite common during the identification process, and it affects any company irrespective of its size. While at first glance, this seems like an issue, in truth, it means that the process was completed successfully.

The recognition of this problem is the point where good stakeholder management needs to take place. This demonstrates that certain things must be done; analysis and prioritization, among others, so as to ensure that the business can utilize its available resources by focusing on the critical stakeholders. At this particular stage, however, the key point is completeness.

Step 2: Identify Key Attributes and Stakeholders

Source: (Hendricks, 2024)

Although it is essential to develop the list of stakeholders, it is important to remember that such an action constitutes only a small portion of good stakeholder management. This is due to the fact that a detailed list will usually contain many stakeholders, and it would be impossible to give the same attention to each one of them. Hence, it is important to focus on the really important ones.

The identification process needs an analysis of the characteristics of the stakeholders. All stakeholders do not hold the same amount of importance, and thus, identifying them will enable effective resource management and involvement in the project. The important stakeholders are those that have considerable influence on the project, a high degree of interest in the project, and are greatly affected by it. There can be instances where stakeholders can become important stakeholders because they present themselves as threats to the project in one way or the other.

In order for this process to take place, it is important that stakeholders are evaluated against certain criteria. Some of the criteria used are: the interest that stakeholders have in the project, how much they are affected by the project, and how much influence they have over the project. Through the evaluation of these characteristics, it will be easier to identify stakeholders that need to be more involved in the project than others.

Tools/systems meant for managing stakeholders can assist in accomplishing this through facilitating systematic analysis and monitoring. These tools will help one capture important aspects of the stakeholders being identified. As a result, it will be possible to classify these stakeholders.

Specifically, measurement of interest assists in identifying the extent to which the stakeholder is involved in the project. The evaluation of impact indicates how much the project would affect the stakeholder, whether positively or negatively. Influence assessment helps measure the capability of the stakeholder to affect the outcome of the project in any way possible.

Stakeholders may also be identified and analyzed at a higher level, thereby enabling a higher level of understanding of their interactions and connections. Through such analysis, companies will be able to recognize the crucial stakeholders who should be accorded priority in the implementation of the project.

In conclusion, finding critical characteristics and interested parties helps turn a generic list into something practical. This process allows organizations to know which people matter the most and why. They can then move forward with more focus and intention, preparing themselves for the next phase.

Step 3: Identifying Key Stakeholders

After understanding the characteristics of the key stakeholders, the next phase would be determining the importance of these stakeholders in a more systematic manner using a visual method. In doing this, stakeholder mapping plays an important part, allowing the organization to convert the data collected from something abstract to something that can be easily understood. Through stakeholder mapping, it is easier to analyze and compare various stakeholders.

The process of stakeholder mapping entails assigning the various characteristics that have been identified into a chart or map. Some of these include interest, influence, and impact. Through such stakeholder maps, the assessment of the stakeholders becomes much easier by identifying how important and relevant they are to the entire context of the stakeholders.

There exist different ways of conducting stakeholder mapping, and each one has its own strengths depending on the situation at hand within the project. Some of the widely used methods include using matrices or grids to depict stakeholders on dimensions such as power or interest. There are other tools, such as Venn diagrams or networks that help to show connections between different stakeholders. Multi-dimensional stakeholder maps take this to another level by including several dimensions at once.

After the mapping process of the stakeholders has been completed, then it becomes feasible to categorize or divide them according to common attributes or relative importance. Such a categorization is necessary in order to come up with a specific strategy to engage them or communicate with them accordingly.

Moreover, apart from the mapping process, there is also an active engagement with stakeholders. Engaging directly with them through dialogues or questionnaires can bring out information that might not have been considered in the first place. By posing pertinent questions, one could find more information about the stakeholders' influences on the project.

Therefore, it is crucial for one to be flexible when it comes to changing the list of stakeholders that will be involved. This is because some of the stakeholders may become new stakeholders while others who were not necessarily important at the start might become increasingly important in the future.

Step 4: Tracking and Analyzing Key Stakeholders

After the identification process of stakeholders is completed, the next step requires appropriate utilization of the gathered information to ensure effective communication with stakeholders and decision-making. It is not sufficient simply to identify stakeholders; rather, there is an additional need to continuously monitor, analyze, and communicate with them. This helps manage stakeholder relations rather than just maintaining them.

More often than not, key stakeholders are likely to demand greater urgency and more strategic involvement than other stakeholders. Owing to their higher degree of influence and impact on the project, it becomes imperative to stay in constant touch with them. As such, it also becomes crucial to maintain records of information relating to such stakeholders.

An effective method involves structuring the stakeholders' files in such a manner that they can be segmented accordingly. Segmenting stakeholders by significance or similar characteristics helps in creating a plan of action. It will become easy for an organization to prioritize its interactions with stakeholders once they have been segmented properly.

Monitoring, apart from planning, is another important step. Engaging monitoring of activities helps to understand if interaction happens as per the schedule and if it is relevant or not. This helps to ensure that communication is still relevant and according to the stakeholders' requirements and project goals. Moreover, it helps companies to ensure that they communicate with the right people frequently enough.

Additional support for the stakeholder analysis process could be provided by using analytical software tools such as dashboards or reports, which help analyze patterns of engagement. The use of these tools allows one to analyze when stakeholders were last engaged, what the engagement was like, and whether there are any shortcomings in that area.

As critical as that is, another equally important activity is collecting and analyzing feedback from stakeholders. Their feedback is very important because of their power and ability to affect the project. Stakeholders' perceptions can be analyzed to determine emerging issues and how satisfied they are with the current engagement process.

The reporting of stakeholder activities and attitudes creates a systematic framework through which an organization can assess its performance and determine how it could improve its practices. This is because, through the analysis of such data, an organization will be able to make informed decisions regarding how it can better its performance.

To conclude, the identification and analysis of critical stakeholders make the stakeholder management approach a continuous process based on the use of data. Organizational efforts can be more effective through the keeping of organized records, stakeholder engagement, and feedback.

1.4 Ethical Principles in AI Systems

The integration of artificial intelligence in organizations has been seen to be a two-edged sword in the contemporary era where there have been tremendous developments in technology. AI bias and automation have been identified as some of the biggest challenges when it comes to the use of AI in innovation and employment, thereby creating a dilemma on whether it should be adopted. There is a need to strike a balance between the potential of AI and its ethical implications. It is indeed true that AI presents numerous opportunities, but it also presents many ethical concerns that should be analyzed in moral terms. It is important for organizations to understand the ethical implications associated with AI. This has been highlighted by the statistics, indicating that at least 25% of organizations have not adopted AI in their strategies. Obviously, the organizations fear AI. It is worth noting that just 38% of the surveyed organizations found AI to be aligned with the organization's ethics.

Source: (Infotech, 2023)

This clearly proves that there is a need to set forth the necessary guidelines for AI usage. The need to pay attention and accept the fact leads to an appropriate attitude. In turn, this is one of the most significant steps towards an ethical approach in using AI technologies. In what follows, we will focus on nine ethical principles about using artificial intelligence that should be considered and accepted with delight in order to go further in this intricate environment in terms of AI technologies usage. In this respect, such principles may become guidelines indicating the ways of implementing AI ethically. Moreover, transparency is becoming a matter of importance in the context of ethical guidelines. Hereby, the fact is proved that 25% of companies now consider the issue of ethics as the top priority point when investing in some AI technologies. On the other hand, 84% of CEOs are convinced that transparency is important to create trust in decision-making by means of AI.

Pillars of Ethical AI

Source: (Infotech, 2023)

1. **Transparency**

   Transparency becomes one of the vital factors when it comes to implementing the nine tenets of ethical use of AI since it is related to the aspect of transparency and honesty. Transparency focuses on the importance of the role of transparency in the field of AI ethics. The significance of transparency calls for firms to offer full explanations regarding the processes involved in the AI software and decision-making processes.

   It also gives room for all the stakeholders to have an opportunity to examine AI-powered decisions. Firms can develop strong pillars of accountability by integrating the use of AI technology with their cultural values. In this regard, it becomes imperative for helping organizations traverse through the ethical dimension of artificial intelligence. This not only helps in mitigating the threats posed by artificial intelligence but also enables organizations to exploit its full potential.

   The importance of transparency will help organizations leverage the power of AI without compromising ethical standards. Organizations can leverage the capabilities of AI technology and use them in a way that upholds ethical standards. In doing so, organizations will be able to ensure that the technology plays a critical role in bringing about positive changes in society in the future. Transparency can be considered the moral pillar on which the AI industry stands, setting the stage for its future success.

2. **Reliability, Robustness and Security**

   Ethics in the utilization of AI technologies is all about security, resilience, and reliability. A study has been conducted highlighting the importance of these factors. The importance of reliable AI technologies comes from the fact that they are reliable, as discussed in this report. It shows the importance of performing activities reliably and precisely for the effective and efficient operation of

AI technologies. It becomes even more important for sectors such as health care and finance, where decisions can be made based on information provided by AI technologies. Employees think that AI increases productivity and satisfaction at work in 82% of cases.

Source: (Infotech, 2023)

Another important aspect discussed in this context is robustness, which increases reliability since it helps tackle the problem related to AI's capacity to address unforeseen problems. According to the research conducted, robust AI technology would be able to regulate itself in case it faces unexpected issues or assaults. This quality not only becomes very useful in terms of constantly developing technologies where the importance of AI increases, but it is also essential if AI is used ethically.

The last feature mentioned in the report is security. The question of protecting AI systems and the data provided by them becomes crucial if one considers the negative effects of the possible security breaches. Among others, one may name invasion into people's private lives and using the technology in committing crimes.

In addition to all previously mentioned qualities, the report suggests that security, robustness, and reliability contribute to one another, creating a basis for the ethical functioning of AI technology. They basically are the committed defender of public trust, prevention of moral hazards, and moral integrity businesses of artificial intelligence.

Those organizations which fully embrace these concepts are definitely going to have an enviable place with regard to artificial intelligence, considering its ever-evolving nature. The organizations shall be in a position to create an AI system whose morality will be flawless, and also it will be one that helps human beings build a solid basis of morality. In effect, the concepts of Reliability, Robustness, and Security will form the key pillars for the ethical use of this AI technology.

3. **Accountability**

Accountability refers to assigning well-defined duties and tasks to each entity involved in the development and application process of AI technologies. It is an important feature since there will be some entity or person who will be accountable for the actions of the AI technology. The question arises as to how we can prevent the misuse of the technology and any harm that may arise from its use.

For example, in the healthcare industry, in addition to developing policies that will promote accountability, organizations need to be responsible for accounting for the harm caused by the deployment of AI technology. This paper analyzes the issues surrounding AI ethics with emphasis on the importance of responsibility.

Transparency is yet another aspect that is crucial for the study of ethics. The level of trust in organizations can be enhanced through transparency in informing its stakeholders about all the duties that they need to perform within the organization concerning artificial intelligence. Transparency is important when it comes to the use of artificial intelligence since everything is done behind closed doors.

4. **Data Privacy**

Data Privacy, which pertains to proper treatment and management of sensitive data, is both a legal and moral obligation when dealing with artificial intelligence. It is due to this reason that:

- **Trust and Consumer Confidence**

  The study found that 60% of consumers show concern about businesses controlling their artificial intelligence system. Data privacy breaches create a trust erosion which proves difficult to restore. Organizations that prioritize data privacy demonstrate to their customers that they treat customer data as highly valuable and secure.

- **Legal and Ethical Compliance**

  Data protection is legally mandatory and not just an ethical consideration. The strict laws that govern the protection of personal information include the California Consumer Privacy Act (CCPA) and the General Data Protection Regulation (GDPR). Organizations that do not adhere risk facing significant fines along with reputational damage and loss of customers.

- **Bias Mitigation**

  AI systems use large datasets for decision-making purposes. The datasets might include bias that perpetuates discrimination and inequalities without data privacy guidelines. It is of the highest importance to safeguard data privacy in order to create AI programs that treat everyone fairly, regardless of their distinct attributes.

- **Innovation and Ethical AI⊠**

  Organizations that put value on data protection will be able to handle the moral quandaries arising from AI effectively since they will find a balance between honoring the rights of individuals and harnessing the information they hold in order to drive innovation. It is crucial for there to be robust data privacy to support ethical AI.

Competitive Advantage

Organizations that have a commitment to privacy can benefit economically as well due to the frequency of privacy infringements and data leaks. Companies that take into consideration the matter of their clients' privacy are more likely to attract customers than companies that do not care about privacy at all.

1. **Lawfulness and Compliance**

   Lawfulness and compliance in relation to artificial intelligence suggest the necessity of running businesses within the boundaries of the laws applicable to the usage of AI. It is both an ethical obligation and a mandatory requirement under the applicable laws.

   AI laws exist in different regions and they govern how artificial intelligence should be utilized. In fact, according to some research, 91% of enterprises working in this industry have already embraced AI technology. However, there is a need to exercise caution when dealing with AI laws since failing to do so could result in a breach of the applicable laws.

   The fact that AI usually uses large databases which consist of sensitive data requires compliance with strict data protection laws. According to GDPR, data security needs to be ensured and AI needs public trust.

   Questions of objectivity and non-discrimination are no less relevant. Objectivity is one of the requirements of the ethics guidelines for the usage of AI technologies. The provisions of anti-discrimination legislation make sure that everyone gets fair and equal treatment. That is why the use of AI should not contribute to any discrimination against some particular groups.

Furthermore, the issue of accountability becomes rather pertinent as technology becomes more autonomous. Adherence to regulations may reduce legal uncertainty about the usage of AI as well as make clear responsibility in cases when there is a need to define the person who committed some actions while using AI.

Adherence to the law concerning the usage of AI gains increasing relevance among many organizations. Three-quarters (78%) of the respondents found it "important" that "AI outputs are fair, safe, and reliable". The legal framework in this area keeps evolving together with the growing prevalence of AI in different areas. Therefore, proper legal processes regarding AI become a necessary element for successful business performance.

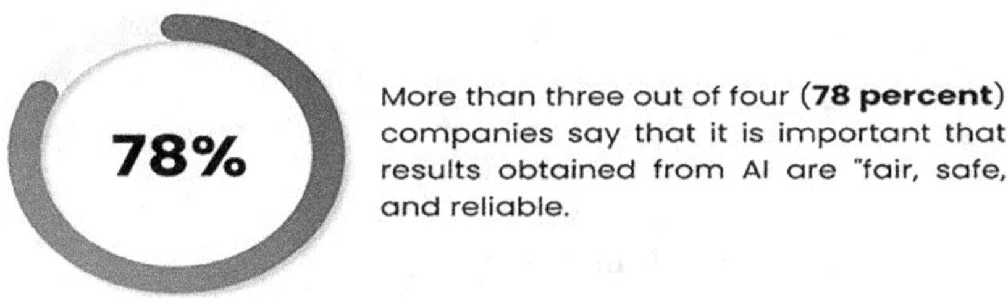

Source: (Infotech, 2023)

2. **Ensuring AI is Sustainable and Beneficial**

   Ethical AI implies the whole process of AI development and use, not just an occasional compliance test. This is why it is so important:

   - **Sustainability**

     The report argues that sustainable development is driven by the ethical application of AI. In this research, it has been brought to light the way AI is able to assist companies in maximizing the utilization of the available resources, thus reducing wastage. Furthermore, through the simulation capability of AI in the evaluation of data for promoting sustainable practices, organizations are able to take eco-conscious measures. It can be said that the concept of ethical AI is very important to develop sustainable AI solutions.

- **Cooperation**

  Ethical AI will foster collaboration and cooperation among business owners, scientists, and politicians. Businesses can cultivate an environment of good practices through their adherence to ethical AI concepts, which will help to enhance AI technologies for all.

- **Openness**

  One of the key elements that should be considered in ethical AI is the issue of transparency. Transparency in the algorithm and availability of data encourage accountability and justice in the AI system. Among those who are expected to trust an AI system is its customers and the wider public, provided it is transparent.

- **Responsible Innovation**

  Ethical AI puts more emphasis on developing AI solutions that are both advanced and ethically acceptable. It compels companies to reflect on how they use their artificial intelligence programs in relation to the effect they have on society regarding things like fairness and privacy. Fair benefits from AI technology are assured through responsible innovation.

- **Trust and Public Acceptance**

  Use of AI technology is highly reliant on trust. Trust will only be gained through the use of ethical approaches to AI.

Organizations that prioritize ethical considerations are likely to gain public support as well as regulatory approval of their AI endeavors.

3. **Human Intervention as Required**

It is important to note that the role of human involvement in ensuring ethical practice in using AI technology in organizations needs to be emphasized, considering that artificial intelligence (AI) is an ever-evolving field. The importance of noting that the level of perceived risk of unethical behavior should inform the extent of human involvement needed during the processes of running an AI technology cannot be ignored. This point has been clearly noted in a recent study conducted on the topic.

Human agency within artificial intelligence involves the necessity of ensuring that humans still maintain a central role in the operation of artificial intelligence processes in any area where ethical concerns abound. Human agency is vital in ensuring that, despite the fact that artificial intelligence processes are very effective, they do not possess the capacity to judge in an ethical manner.

AI models may unwittingly replicate any prejudice present within the data used to train them. Human intervention is necessary to ensure fairness in AI outcomes, as it helps detect and mitigate bias. Companies need to manage any potential sources of bias that could lead to discrimination.

Ethical risks related to different AI uses differ. Understanding the degree of ethical risk enables us to determine the right amount of human agency that must be exercised. More human agency is needed in making important decisions in the areas of self-driving vehicles and medicine to ensure ethics and safety. In the case of the judgment being made by the AI, human agency provides a chain of accountability for that action. Locating the individuals to be held responsible for the outcome is vital.

All stakeholders have increased confidence in the operation of artificial intelligence systems with human supervision. This ensures that decisions made are understandable and explainable, as it provides insights into the process used by the artificial intelligence system to make such decisions. Humans can identify where the weaknesses of artificial intelligence lie and improve accordingly.

However, human agency must be a key element of ethical application of AI in companies; it should not be seen as an obstacle. Human agency and the associated risks may be used to strike a balance between making full use of the possibilities of AI and maintaining the company's integrity. The ability to see the significance of human involvement is vital for ethical implementation of AI in today's world where AI becomes ever more ubiquitous. This will help ensure that AI serves ethical development and transformation, benefiting both companies and people worldwide.

4. **Safety**

AI safety is a complicated idea in the sense that it takes into consideration the safety and well-being of individuals from both physical and psychological perspectives within the entire lifespan of an AI system. This means that AI safety focuses on the duty of companies to ensure that there is no danger posed by the technology to individuals. The findings of the study reinforce the notion of AI safety.

Source: (Infotech, 2023)

- **Physical Safety**

  The AI technology has the capability to influence the physical security of humans. This occurs when the AI system is integrated into machinery and vehicles such as autonomous cars. Therefore, the importance of ensuring the security of individuals utilizing the AI technology is paramount. The paper mostly explains why strong measures should be taken to safeguard the errors of AI.

- **Mental Well-being**

  There could also be another effect related to psychological factors apart from the one related to physical safety associated with the use of AI. The possible negative impact of AI could be linked to its misuse and incorrect decision-making because of AI algorithms. This problem highlights the importance of avoiding such a negative outcome.

- **Ethical Dilemmas**

  The mental health of man could be adversely impacted by the ethics issue related to artificial intelligence. The current study focuses on the significance for companies to consider such ethical issues, taking into account the mental health of man.

- **Public Trust**

  In order for one to be able to win the trust of individuals in artificial intelligence technologies, safety has to be a concern. Individuals will be willing to embrace technology if they know that there is safety concerned. When firms make safety a priority, they not only do the right thing but also create long-term business relationships.

  AI reportedly has substantial implications for the well-being and safety of the general population. The organizations maintain ethical integrity and promote the creation of an ethically sound environment with the use of AI technology through prioritizing safety at every stage of the development of AI technology. Safety should be considered as an ethical requirement for full exploitation of the benefits of AI technology.

5. **Fairness**

   Several ethical theories also suggest that fairness means that AI tools must give equal treatment to individuals within the same groups without being biased towards any of them, nor doing harm. In this case, fairness refers to ensuring that all people have equal treatment during their entire journey from creation to implementation.

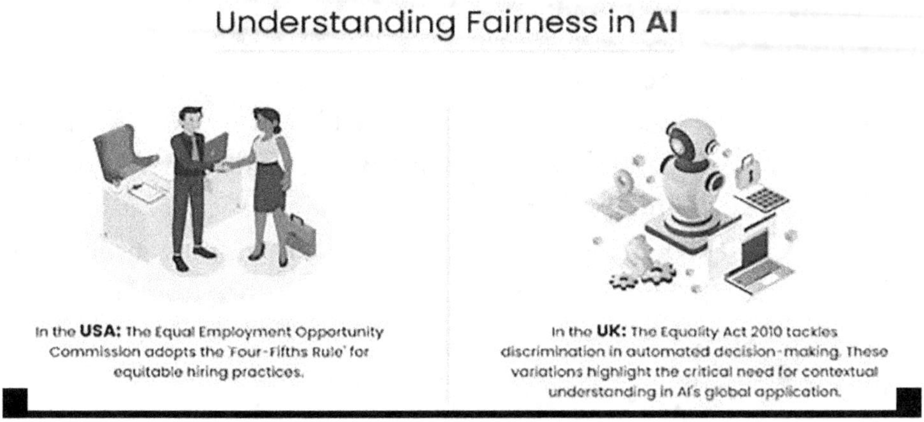

Source: (Infotech, 2023)

- **Mitigating Discriminatory Biases**

  In order for AI algorithms to make decisions, they use huge amounts of data. The problem is that such a dataset can contain hidden biases that might foster discriminatory practices. It is imperative that companies detect them consciously.

- **Respect for Individual Privacy**

  The respect for the dignity of individuals who supply information to an AI system is yet another form of fairness. Organizations must provide security for the data that they use and prevent individuals' private information from intrusion and exploited.

- **Addressing Ethical Dilemmas**

  The principle of fairness assumes great significance in the complex milieu of artificial intelligence since it is imperative to strike a fine balance while resolving ethical dilemmas in the wake of decisions made by artificial intelligence. Artificial intelligence encounters scenarios where competing values prevail.

- **Trust and Public Perception**

  Apart from the moral justification for fairness, it acts as a tool through which trust can be established between the parties involved, such as clients, employees, and the general public. In establishing trust towards AI, it is important to portray a sense of accountability and transparency. By ensuring justice above everything else, companies guarantee their commitment to ethical standards and present AI positively.

1.5 Global AI Governance Frameworks and Standards

AI technologies have attained some level of importance in key areas like governance, health sector, financial sector and so forth. It is important to note that the need for good governance in these technological aspects has emerged. Governance in this sense is defined as an organized structure consisting of policies and processes within the organization.

AI governance systems rely on concepts such as accountability, transparency, interpretability, and fairness. Furthermore, they help corporations create frameworks for managing risks, compliance, and trust issues. It is necessary to mention that AI governance frameworks are sufficiently flexible, which allows corporations to adjust their AI policies according to local laws and cultures.

Importance of AI Governance Frameworks

These AI governance models do not only emphasize AI alignment to ethical principles but also the mitigation of operational risks. Operational risks that businesses may encounter when adopting AI technology could include algorithmic discrimination, inappropriate data utilization, lack of transparency, and privacy risks.

The importance of AI governance can be summarized in the following ways:

Why AI Governance Matters	What It Enables
Reduces Immediate Risks	Prevents bias, data misuse, and privacy breaches.
Establishes Clear Principles	Provides structured guidelines for responsible AI use.
Improves System Transparency	Promotes explainability, fairness, and accountability.
Aligns Team Understanding	Ensures shared clarity on AI goals, risks, and responsibilities.
Builds Stakeholder Trust	Shows internal and external audiences a commitment to security and compliance.

Source: (Ai2i, 2025)

Additional benefits include:

- Frameworks have norms for the right use of AI technology in business operations.
- Through a framework, an organization is able to establish criteria on accountability, transparency, and fairness in their AI applications.
- Having such a framework put in place means that there is common understanding within various departments regarding AI goals, limitations, and control.
- By using an AI governance framework, the organization shows its stakeholders that it has formal procedures for the safety and compliance of their AI implementations.

What are the key principles behind AI governance frameworks?

Across the various AI principles, orders, and standards—some of which are outlined in later sections—several common themes emerge in responsible AI governance.

- **Human oversight:** AI systems must remain under meaningful human control.
- **Transparency:** Users and regulators should be able to understand how an AI system generates outputs or decisions.
- **Accountability:** There must be clearly defined responsibility for AI outcomes.
- **Safety:** Systems should be secure, reliable, and resilient to failures or adversarial attacks.
- **Fairness and non-discrimination:** AI should be developed and applied to mitigate bias and support equitable treatment.
- **Privacy and data protection:** AI must uphold individuals' data rights and comply with applicable data protection laws.
- **Proportionality:** Oversight and intervention should correspond to the potential impact of the AI system.
- **Human-centric design:** AI should support human well-being and align with fundamental rights.

Various frameworks lay emphasis on different principles. For instance, gender equality and environmental sustainability are given more attention in the UNESCO Recommendation on the Ethics of Artificial Intelligence.

The AI systems fall under the European Union AI Act to classify them as unacceptable, high, limited, or little risk, providing a tiered risk-based classification system. This arrangement is not found in most other governance systems, and has explicit restrictions on some of the high risk use.

Key Legal and Regulatory AI Governance Frameworks for 2025

Companies can design AI systems that are ethical, safe, and aligned with both domestic and international law through the use of laws and regulations. Some of the laws and regulations mentioned below will assist in designing such an AI system:

1. **EU AI Act:**

   An EU AI Act is a legally binding law that splits AI systems into four categories of danger unacceptable, high, limited, and low.

   It imposes strict limitations to applications that are high-risk, including financial service and healthcare, and prohibits certain uses, including social scoring. Companies that work in the European Union face harsh fines in the event that they fail to comply with this model.

2. **UK Pro-Innovation AI Framework**

   The five pillars of the UK pro-innovation AI framework are fairness, transparency, accountability, safety, and contestability, which is a non-statutory whitepaper.

   It particularly fits the companies that need regulatory consistency without excessive compliance costs since it is a flexible, situation-specific method.

3. **Executive Orders on AI (United States)**

   During the presidency of Biden, the United States published the Executive Order 14110. It released an Executive order 14179 in 2025 with the title of Removing Barriers to American Leadership in Artificial Intelligence.

   These orders provide federal regulation of AI usage in such spheres as public services, national security, and civil rights. They are particularly anxious about keeping the global lead in AI and not to prejudge and influence systems wrongly.

4. **NIST AI Risk Management Framework (AI RMF)**

   NIST AI Risk Management Framework provides risk-based guidelines on how to build and deploy trustworthy AI systems.

   It is premised upon four basic functions that include govern, map, measure, and manage and is widely applied in a wide variety of industries.

5. **AI Bill of Rights**

   The AI Bill of Rights is an initiative that was published by the White House Office of Science and Technology Policy in 2022; it is not obligatory from a legal perspective.

   It presents some of the fundamental ideas, including the confidentiality of information, equity, and human management, and it has shaped the further regulatory activities in the US.

6. **U.S. State-Level Regulations**

   The AI law at the state level is evolving rapidly and is considered a legal obligation in some regions in the US.

   An example is the AI Act of Colorado (CAIA), which prohibits high-risk systems that are based on algorithms and apply them in education, healthcare, and employment. The currently introduced Automated Decision Systems Accountability Act of California is also aimed at enhancing accountability and transparency in decision-making with AI.

7. **OECD AI Principles**

   Human-centered, transparent, and accountable AI development is encouraged by the OECD AI Principles, which are non-binding international standards.

First presented in 2019 and revised in 2024, the principles have enjoyed widespread acceptance, particularly among the OECD member countries.

8. **UNESCO AI Ethics Framework**

   The UNESCO Recommendation on the Ethics of Artificial Intelligence is the first international standard of AI ethics.

   It is a voluntary agreement of the member states of the UN that places high emphasis on compliance to human rights, sustainability, and inclusivity.

9. **G7 Code of Conduct for Advanced AI (2023)**

   This self-regulatory model, developed by the G7 nations, outlines exemplary practices of the responsible and safe creation of advanced AI systems, such as generative AI.

   It supports the larger G7 Action Plan, which encourages member nations to deploy safe, human-centered AI.

How to Select an Enterprise AI Governance Structure

When it comes to ensuring the alignment of AI projects to business objectives and ensuring the maintenance of security, ethical standards, and compliance with regulations, selecting the appropriate governance architecture is essential.

Category	What to Focus On
Policies & Procedures	Define clear rules for data quality, privacy, model development, deployment, and monitoring.
Governance Ownership	Assign roles
Strategic Alignment	Align with business priorities
Security & Compliance	Prioritize secure infrastructure
Design Phase	Deploy in secure environments with audit logs, access control, and issue reporting processes.
Monitoring Phase	Use dashboards, feedback loops, and retraining pipelines to adapt to evolving data and usage.
Ongoing Risk Management	Run regular audits, track drift, bias, and performance drops; act before failures occur.
Explainability	Use tools like execution graphs, confidence scores, and reasoning chains to ensure transparency.

Source: (Ai2i, 2025)

- **Develop your own clear policies and procedures**

  Establishing standards for data quality and privacy and model development and implementation and ongoing monitoring. The Operations publishes guidelines for teams to comply in incorporating AI technologies into their operations.

- **Establish a formal governance structure**

  Designated ownership is necessary for AI governance. The project requires the identification of data stewards who will manage data quality while AI leaders execute their work and compliance officers address all regulatory matters, and the team will build systems for collecting end-user feedback to support their development process.

- **Align with strategic priorities**

  The overarching objectives of your organization should be supported by your governance structures. The development of healthcare and banking industries requires organizations to build their systems with accuracy and transparency as permanent features. The evaluation of AI decisions requires the implementation of execution graphs and explainability layers and audit logs.

- **Build in security and compliance**

  The cornerstones should be security and regulatory compliance. Organizations need to use virtual private cloud (VPC) technology through private deployment options or on-premises system solutions to control their data access and model performance and system security in secure environments.

- **Implementation guidance for AI governance frameworks**

  Artificial intelligence governance should extend through all phases of a company's system development, which begins at system design and continues through system implementation, system observation and system maintenance. This guide aims to outline a structured method to operationalize an organization's AI governance framework.

- **Design phase**

  Before development starts teams need to create a functional map which shows all AI system functions and their enterprise use cases during the design stage. The process needs to establish traceability methods along with regulatory compliance procedures and model performance standards at its initial stage.

The system can be tested for different conditions and its edge cases can be identified through simulations that use training data to create real-world testing environments.

- **Deployment phase**

  AI technologies need to be rolled out in a secure setting such as VPCs and on-premises environments. This is possible from the onset through the inclusion of audit logs, output validation methods, and access controls. It is essential for an organization to foster internal reporting on risks that violate responsible AI standards and even consider incentives.

- **Monitoring phase**

  Monitoring dashboards and the collection of user feedback through an organized process must be implemented in order to retain observability throughout the monitoring process. Automatic training will enable model adaptation because data distribution and application scenarios will undergo changes. The system requires ongoing monitoring to ensure compliance with regulatory standards.

- **Ongoing risk management**

  However, Risk Management tools must be sufficiently proactive to address biases, drifts, and degradation risks. It is essential to regularly audit your organization to ensure compliance with the latest regulations to act as a risk manager.

- **Explain ability and observability**

  Transparency to be built between explainability and observability of the system, execution graphs, together with confidence levels and reasoning paths should accompany the system. This is because the regulated industries require means of assessing the performance of AI in order to ensure that the results generated are accountable and trustworthy by all parties.

Principles and standards of responsible AI governance

Gen AI is something that will inform the AI governance with recommended oversight mechanisms. There are a wide range of potential applications for generative AI, which encompasses technology that can produce fresh material and solutions including writing, graphics, and code.

Generative AI is changing how industries function, from improving creative processes in design and media to automating activities in software development. However, strong AI governance is required due to its wide applicability.

Organizations must adhere to the principles of responsible AI governance in order to protect both themselves and their clients. These guidelines, which include the following, can help organizations create and use AI technologies in an ethical manner:

- **Empathy:** Organizations should understand the societal implications of AI, not just the technological and financial aspects. They need to anticipate and address the impact of AI on all stakeholders.
- **Bias control:** It is essential to rigorously examine training data to prevent embedding real-world biases into AI algorithms, helping to ensure fair and unbiased decision-making processes.
- **Transparency:** There must be clarity and openness in how AI algorithms operate and make decisions, with organizations ready to explain the logic and reasoning behind AI-driven outcomes.
- **Accountability:** Organizations should proactively set and adhere to high standards to manage the significant changes AI can bring, maintaining responsibility for AI's impacts.

Organizations must still decide how to balance these criteria for their business, even while market forces and legislation standardize many governance metrics. Each organization must determine which emphasis areas to target in order to measure the effectiveness of AI governance. It is not a one-size-fits-all choice with focus areas like data quality, model security, cost-value analysis, bias monitoring, individual accountability, ongoing auditing, and flexibility to adapt based on the organization's domain (Carlton, 2024).

Multiple Choice Questions (MCQs)

1. **What is the primary purpose of AI governance?**

   A. To increase AI speed

   B. To ensure ethical, safe, and responsible use of AI

   C. To replace human decision-making

   D. To reduce data storage costs

2. **Which of the following best defines AI governance?**

   A. Designing AI algorithms only

   B. Managing AI hardware systems

   C. Frameworks, policies, and processes guiding AI development and use

   D. Programming AI models

3. **What is a key reason AI governance has become important?**

   A. Increased gaming applications

   B. Growing concerns about bias, privacy, and accountability

   C. Decrease in data availability

   D. Reduction in AI usage

4. **Which historical phase marked the beginning of formal AI regulation?**

   A. Early computing era (1950s)

   B. Industrial revolution

   C. Rise of modern AI and data-driven systems (21st century)

   D. Pre-internet era

5. **Who are considered key stakeholders in AI governance?**

   A. Only software developers

   B. Governments, organizations, developers, and users

   C. Only data scientists

   D. Only private companies

6. **Which stakeholder is primarily responsible for creating AI regulations?**

   A. End users

   B. Governments and regulatory bodies

   C. Software engineers

   D. Customers

7. **Which ethical principle ensures AI decisions can be understood and explained?**

   A. Privacy

   B. Transparency

   C. Scalability

   D. Automation

8. **What does fairness in AI systems aim to achieve?**

   A. Faster computations

   B. Equal treatment and avoidance of bias

   C. Higher profits

   D. More data collection

9. **Which of the following is an example of a global AI governance framework?**

   A. Social media policies

   B. OECD AI Principles

   C. Local company rules

   D. Gaming regulations

10. **What is a major challenge in global AI governance?**

    A. Lack of computing devices

    B. Differences in regulations across countries

    C. Too many programming languages

    D. Limited internet access

Answers

1	2	3	4	5	6	7	8	9	10
B	C	B	C	B	B	B	B	B	B

Chapter 2

Building Trustworthy AI Systems

2.1 Defining Trust in Artificial Intelligence

Trustworthy AI refers to artificial intelligence systems that are transparent, safe, secure, robust, egalitarian, explainable, and interpretable. These characteristics give stakeholders and end users faith in AI systems.

The possible hazards connected to the use of AI models can be reduced by trustworthy artificial intelligence, or TAI. These concerns associated with AI include damage to individuals, institutions, and ecosystems. Such damages have the potential to erode confidence in artificial intelligence in general as well as in particular AI models.

Reliable AI frameworks can assist enterprises in developing, implementing, and assessing AI technology. The Organization for Economic Co-operation and Development (OECD), the European Commission's High-Level Expert Group on AI, and the US National Institute of Standards and Technology (NIST) have established such frameworks (Lu, Zhu, Whittle, & Xu, 2023).

Why is trustworthy AI important?

Trusting the effectiveness of a technology generally requires an understanding of how it operates. However, many machines learning (ML) and artificial intelligence (AI) systems, including deep learning models, are black boxes that load data and output findings without explanation.

As a result, there are many gaps in trust. According to a 2023 poll, over 40% of corporate executives expressed doubts about the reliability of AI. In the meantime, customers have also shown mistrust of AI: a 2024 study discovered that labeling a product with the term "artificial intelligence" may discourage buyers from purchasing it.

Concerns about AI trust are further stoked by real-world instances of AI systems generating incorrect or detrimental outcomes in high-stakes use cases. The use of an AI model failed to diagnose sepsis in a famous case in medicine. The algorithm was capable of detecting sepsis in over two-thirds of hospital patients even though it works well in a training setting.

In others, when AI-based hiring mechanisms favor men above women and policing algorithms target minority groups unfairly, bias in AI has been witnessed. The other case is the issue of cybersecurity, where there is the misuse of AI chatbots to disclose confidential data and attackers to use weaknesses in AI models to steal sensitive corporate data.

Mistakes and poor performance of AI models may cause a negative perception of the models and AI in general, potentially reducing the pace of its further evolution and application. The concept of the black box of AI is important in order to create reliable AI systems and contribute to its further evolution. This makes it less likely that AI systems would generate biased or unintended results, giving stakeholders more faith in the accuracy and reliability of the data they receive.

What are the principles of trustworthy AI?

The ideas and objectives for trustworthy AI are emphasized differently by different frameworks and organizations. Here are a few commonly mentioned concepts of reliable AI:

- **Accountability**

  The proper functioning of AI systems throughout the lifespan of AI actors is an important part of AI accountability. This comprises people and institutions engaged in creating, implementing, or using AI technology.

- **Explain ability**

  The goal of AI explain ability is to validate or provide explanations for a model's results. In the context of machine learning, "explainable AI" is a suite of methods for making algorithm outputs more understandable and trustworthy for human users.

- **Fairness**

  When we say that an AI is unbiased or that an AI is fair, we simply refer to the fact that the AI treats people and groups of people fairly. One aspect of ensuring fairness is ensuring that there are no biases in the algorithms used and, in the data, used to train them. Artificial intelligence models can exhibit both data bias and algorithmic bias.

- **Interpretability and transparency**

  AI models' decision-making processes become easier to comprehend and explain through AI interpretability. Transparency of the architecture, characteristics, and decision-making process of an AI model is what defines its interpretability. While there are some models whose operations can be understood without interpreting them, others require them to be interpreted.

- **Privacy**

  The concept of privacy in AI entails making sure that there are no PII that get collected, processed, disclosed, and retained via AI. Privacy of data and AI privacy are both intertwined concepts. The right of an individual to control his or her personal information is referred to as the data privacy or information privacy. A number of strategies, such as encryption, may be considered in improving AI privacy and data privacy.

- **Reliability**

  Reliability refers to the ability to function as desired for a particular period of time in a particular environment without failing in any way. When used properly, reliable AI systems should be able to deliver accurate results within a particular period of time, which could even cover their entire lifespan.

- **Robustness and security**

  In order to reduce cybersecurity risks and vulnerabilities, secure and resilient AI systems have safeguards in place to prevent hostile attacks and illegal access. They can continue functioning normally following an unanticipated incident and can even operate in unusual environments without harming anyone.

- **Safety**

  Protected AI systems do not pose any threat to people, animals, or the natural world. They take precautions to prevent harm to individuals and incorporate safeguards to lessen the impact of bad things happening, such as the option to disable a system.

What risks can trustworthy AI mitigate?

Artificial intelligence systems that aren't trustworthy are dangerous in many ways. A paradigm that has established a benchmark for AI risk management was developed by the National Institute of Standards and Technology (NIST), which is part of the US Department of Commerce. It classifies the possible dangers posed by AI systems into subcategories:

- **Harm to people**

  Threats to people's physical or mental well-being, economic opportunities, civil rights, and freedoms fall under this category. In addition to effects on individuals, this includes societal effects such as barriers to democratic participation and educational opportunities, as well as effects on groups through prejudice.

- **Harm to an organization**

  In this group, we find damages to a company's reputation, security breaches, and financial losses or disruptions to its commercial activities.

- **Harm to an ecosystem**

  Damage to "interconnected and interdependent elements and resources" falls under this heading. Threats to natural resources, the environment, and the world's financial and supply chains are among the many "interrelated systems" listed by NIST.

  There are a lot of problems that might arise when AI systems produce biased or misleading results. Going back to a previous example, biased applicant-tracking systems can impact both the reputation of the company and the economic potential of people. It would be disastrous for the organization and its supply chain if an LLM could be deceived into executing malware that cripples' operations.

  Possible solutions to these catastrophic outcomes could lie in trustworthy AI systems. "Reliable AI systems and their responsible use can mitigate negative risks and contribute to benefits for people, organizations and ecosystems," goes the National Institute of Standards and Technology's official statement.

2.2 Fairness, Bias, and Non-Discrimination

Integrity, objectivity, and absence of discrimination are the pillars of AI regulation. It is essential to guarantee that artificial intelligence technologies operate objectively and without discrimination on a moral and regulatory basis, given their significance in making decisions in various sectors such as health care, policing, and finance.

Bias in AI

Machine learning models that reproduce and exacerbate any underlying biases inherent in the data can contribute to systematic injustices that are termed as "bias within AI systems." Bias within AI systems arises from algorithmic influence on social justice where algorithms produce biased results because of bad data or bad development choices. Using data that is already biased during the development of an algorithm leads to reproduction of the pre-existing prejudices.

AI bias affects the objectiveness and precision of machine learning algorithms. Some people may be victims of injustice and unfairness simply because we failed to address our biases in these AI technologies. If fairness is to be maintained, then it is important to do something about our biases.

If the goal is to make sure that AI operates fairly and justly for everyone irrespective of which group they belong to, it is important to identify and remove such biases.

How AI Systems Develop Bias

AI systems are prone to bias based on their design, datasets, and decision-making process. In instances where an AI system makes decisions on new data sets, they can produce erroneous information because of bias already present in the datasets. Bias can be introduced in an AI system during its development through different stages, including data collection, labeling, training, and implementation. Ensuring that an AI system works equitably among different demographies can be challenging; human biases associated with classifying data and defining fairness metrics can exacerbate the problem. An AI system will deliver biased outcomes on certain demographies if datasets are homogenous.

AI models' decisions are often biased as they use implicit bias that may exist in their datasets, but which they may not be aware of. The issue of selection bias occurs due to the fact that the datasets being used for training AI models fail to represent the real world. In doing so, they produce biased outcomes for certain individuals. Thus, the accuracy of predictions is compromised. Relying on existing biases can prevent an AI model from recognizing new patterns if it falls into confirmation bias.

One of the potential sources of bias may be the existence of an ongoing difference between real-world figures and data collected for the purpose of AI; the said difference may greatly influence how certain demographic groups are analyzed. Tackling bias and reducing its consequences is imperative to make decisions based on AI fair. This ensures that all AI systems remain unbiased in any scenario.

Real-world examples of AI Bias

The algorithms employed for credit scoring can be biased against individuals belonging to particular socio-economic groups due to bias in data sets. The data set bias could play a significant role in the opportunities of individuals, as is illustrated in the following example. Studies reveal that facial recognition algorithms are much more prone to error when identifying people with dark skin color than those with light skin color. In a study conducted at MIT Media Lab, it was found that dark-skinned women were misidentified 34.7 percent of the time while white men were misidentified just 0.8 percent of the time.

The use of artificial intelligence in the hiring process may increase pre-existing biases in the workplace, where preference is given to words that are predominantly used by men, thereby reducing the opportunities for women. Recruiting processes using artificial intelligence have inherent biases towards some groups as there is an absence of diverse data sets. A lack of fairness in the recruiting process could be a consequence of the algorithms replicating gender discrimination patterns in the previous workforce data sets based on past hiring decisions. The recruiting process at Amazon involving an algorithm is an example, as it showed discriminatory patterns towards males due to the predominance of male preferences in résumé data.

Selection bias becomes a concern if the data used does not reflect the target population accurately, resulting in poor predictive power from models. There is also confirmation bias as an issue within AI, whereby the system puts too much emphasis on existing trends. This shows how important it is to detect any possible biases in a data set and work out ways of correcting them.

Source: (Tarud, 2025)

Types of AI Bias

There are several types of biases that an AI system can be biased towards hence influencing the efficacy of the model. To counter these issues, it is important to be aware of the different forms of biases in AI, such as algorithmic biases, sample biases, and labeling biases. Some of the most common forms of biases in AI include:

Each type has different characteristics, which influence the performance of machine learning algorithms. The prediction capability of the model is likely to lack generalizability if the training set does not capture enough variation within the population. This happens as a result of sampling bias. Conversely, labeling bias refers to the problem where training samples contain mislabeled data.

In addition to that, skewness in data may arise from systematic errors while collecting the data, thus making the next research invalid. Likewise, discrimination using algorithmic bias is where the algorithm is deliberately used to produce biased outcomes.

- **Sample Bias**

  Sample bias takes place when the data sets fail to appropriately represent the population and hence give rise to incorrect and inconsistent results obtained from these models. Incorporation of representation bias in such a scenario might have a profound effect on the accuracy of results generated by AI systems. A practical example can be drawn from the fact that use of AI by people outside its representative demographic group may affect its performance.

  It is essential that varied data be used when training an AI system in order to counter sampling bias effectively. Data collected from different demographics should also be taken into consideration when training these models since it would ensure that they become fairer and more accurate in nature.

- **Label Bias**

  AI systems are vulnerable to label bias when the labels within a dataset are inaccurate or discriminatory, suggesting that the data lack representation. Gender and race discrimination can significantly influence machine learning outcomes, and therefore, a good example of this would be that it is highly likely that the AI systems generated will produce outputs that are inherently prejudiced towards gender and race.

  Another strategy for removing label bias is applying a confident learning approach to check label accuracy and rule out samples that have biased labels. To detect possible instances of bias, one could generate and contrast predictions using multiple AI models trained on different data sets.

Organizations looking for more precision in their AI model must have strict labeling criteria and also seek consistency among multiple annotators on something. Such a practice has the potential to significantly minimize label bias and help machine learning algorithms deliver better performance.

- **Measurement Bias**

  Measurement bias takes place when the measurements or the means by which information is gathered systematically distort the raw data. For example, if an AI algorithm was fed information based on only the performance of students who had successfully completed a class, it might fail to determine how well those who dropped out of school would fare. Measurement bias arises due to such differences, and such bias might cause substantial variations when AI models assess individuals based on their demographics.

  However, to resolve any inconsistencies with the data, it is essential to collect information using methods that yield a wide range of samples that correctly represent the variables under consideration. In order for AI to produce unbiased results, it is essential to apply appropriate and objective criteria.

- **Algorithmic Bias**

  "Algorithmic bias" refers to the case whereby an algorithm generates consistent biased or discriminatory results due to either its programming or execution. "Fairness" is a core consideration for AI results; however, fairness might not always prevail when the results generated by the algorithm show signs of discrimination, affecting some communities differently than others. An example of such an effect would be when the algorithm is programmed on false assumptions.

  Making an AI fair requires finding the source of computational bias behind the discrimination of demographic groups. Algorithms, data used in algorithms, and the broader impact of all the mentioned aspects on society require thorough investigation during this process. To ensure fairness and equity of AI, it is necessary to understand why such systems are biased and correct this flaw.

Fairness in AI

It is very crucial that all demographics are treated fairly and the AI system does not discriminate against any group. Ensuring that the systems' outputs do not discriminate against any individual, e.g. on the basis of personal characteristics such as gender, race, and socio-economic status, is very important.

Ensuring AI fairness is really a tough task as it means integrating various moral views by relying on recognized fairness standards.

Actually, the safeguarding of fairness, along with adherence to community norms by the AI system, calls for ongoing watchfulness to tackle any kind of prejudices.

Defining Fairness in Machine Learning

One of the things that distinguishes different fairness approaches in machine learning is the kind of relationship that AI should have with the user. Equality, equity, and justice are just a few of the perspectives. Most of the approaches take the lead from decision-making through the inclusion of the different demographic groups. A shining example of fair AI would be something along the lines of making sure that discriminating a group based on such factors as ethnicity or gender does not happen.

Applying fairness measures consistently to different AI applications is difficult without a generally accepted notion of fairness in machine learning algorithms. The reason for this is that something considered fair in one scenario may be seen as unfair in another. The lack of a universal standard has made it very challenging to build an AI that can always display fairness.

In order to get a more precise method of judging the fairness of something, some researchers have devised indicators that work on the basis of the likelihood of the occurrence of a given event versus the expected outcome. Having such an instrument at our disposal, we are now able to engage in an advanced discourse on the subject of fairness. Major contributions to the achievement of greater fairness among different demographic groups, as well as the lessening of their stigmatization, refer to methods that at first uncover and then increase the alignment between the sensitive characteristics of machine learning systems and the predictions resulting from them.

Key Metrics for Measuring AI Fairness

AI decision-making algorithms must be designed to make sure that every demographic group is given equal chances of benefiting from the decisions. In this way, the decision-making process becomes fair and unbiased. Such a fairness standard would be extremely useful, especially when it comes to employment and credit applications, where it is highly undesirable for the AI to have any form of bias.

The reason for having equal opportunity metrics is to ensure that individuals from diverse backgrounds will not be discriminated against in any way while striving for good results. Achieving predictive parity aims to guarantee that different demographic groups will experience the same degree of accuracy when forecasting their outcomes. Using this metric alone, can we assess if our AI predictions are correct?

The equality of odds rule is intended to ensure that true positives and false positives are equally distributed among different groups. In order to expose all types of biases in one dataset, it is necessary to apply multiple bias fairness measures.

It's crucial to incorporate these bias fairness standards as they assist in revealing and tackling biases in AI models. Through these materials, companies will understand ways to deal with the problem of fairness in AI deployment.

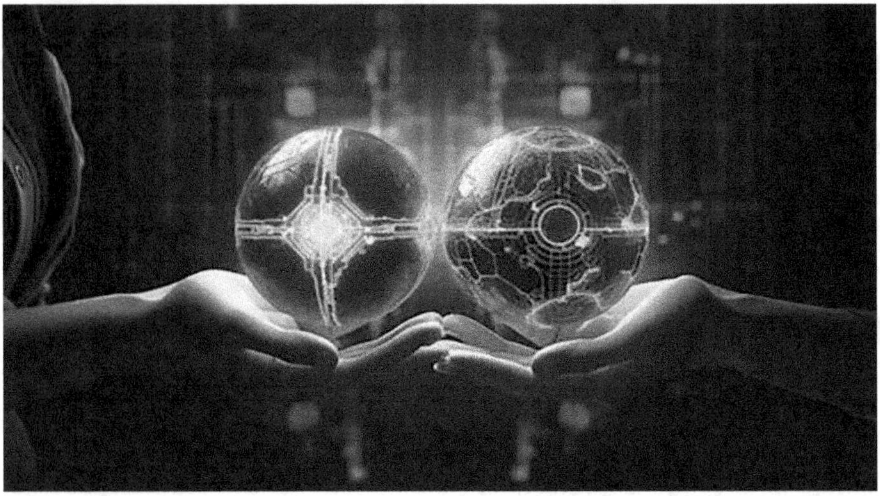

Source: (Tarud, 2025)

Real-World Cases of AI Bias and Fairness Issues

It is necessary to solve the identified challenges promptly to ensure that the process of implementing AI technologies is fair. This statement is true as several cases of bias in AI have been found. There are many such examples, and they demonstrate why it is essential to identify and eliminate any biases present in the AI systems. Many areas may be affected by the identified biases including algorithms applied to making decisions about people's health or the use of facial recognition technology.

The following discussion will focus on specific examples of the application of AI technologies when biases may occur during medical treatment, recruitment, and facial recognition.

1. **AI Bias in Facial Recognition**

   Research has proved that facial recognition technology isn't flawless, especially when it comes to identifying individuals from oppressed races. In case the database used by the algorithm predominantly contains images of Caucasian individuals, the results will be significantly biased. It's clear from the huge difference in the error rates of the two categories that the system has a tendency to misidentify dark-skinned females at a rate of 34.7%, while white males are misidentified just 0.8% of the time.

   A facial recognition tool capable of making accurate assessments would contribute to growing the gap of racial inequality in the area of law enforcement. Given that such technology isn't flawless, there are instances where innocent people get wrongly detained due to flaws. Such scenarios raise concerns over how such technology could be abused and compromise the constitutional rights of Americans.

2. **AI Bias in Hiring and Recruitment**

   Gender discrimination against female applicants via artificial intelligence (AI) algorithms employed in the recruiting process may be because of the bias embedded in AI training datasets due to gender imbalance in the workforce. After discovering that their AI hiring algorithm was biased against women, Amazon discontinued use of this tool. The algorithm ranks female-associated terms less favorably on resumes compared to the male- associated terms because of its training dataset consisting mostly of male hiring applications. The potential danger that such AI could perpetuate existing workplace biases is apparent from this.

   The remedy that businesses have resorted to is the use of auditing software to assess the fairness of AI-driven recruiting algorithms to ensure that a wide range of applicants is considered. The significance of fairness metrics in determining the success of recruiting processes based on technological solutions is increasingly being recognized by businesses.

3. **AI Bias in Healthcare**

   However, inadequate representation of minority groups within healthcare AI poses an increased probability of unintentional bias transfer through recommendations for unequal treatment. A popular AI tool used in healthcare could have potentially caused harm if the results were followed because it underestimated the healthcare needs of African-Americans relative to White recipients as explained in a study published in science.

   Diverse patient information in data sets can go a long way in reducing these issues. A medical expert who bases their decisions on such comprehensive data sets can give unbiased treatment suggestions.

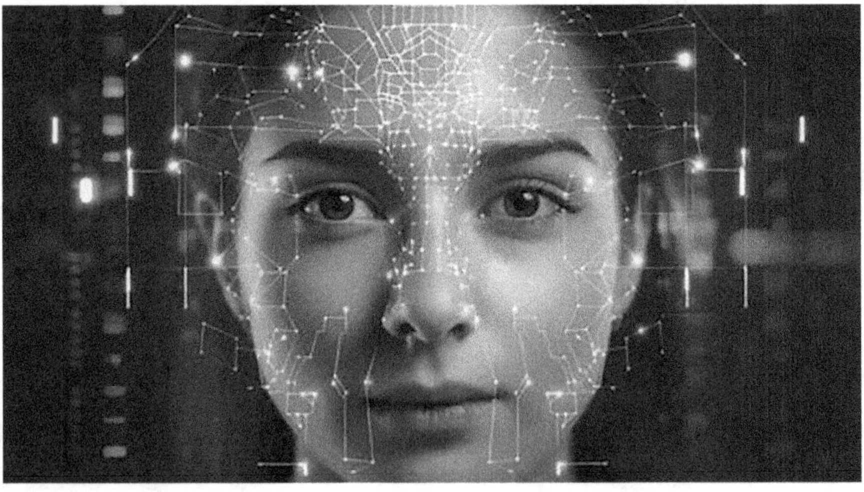

Source: (Tarud, 2025)

Strategies to Reduce AI Bias and Improve Fairness

In order to build AI models with ethical awareness, steps must be taken not only to curb AI bias but also to work on problems of fairness and promote equity. Part of such methods involve using diverse ways of data gathering, designing algorithms with fairness in mind, and regularly auditing AI systems for fairness and equity. By being up front about these biases, companies will be able to realize fairness and justice in their AI implementations.

This section will discuss some of the strategies to mitigate AI bias. The discussion will include some methods used in diverse data collection and pre-processing, algorithms that promote equity, and an ethics-guided AI operations audit.

- **Data Collection and Preprocessing**

  One way to abolish stale biases impacting AI decision-making is to ensure that datasets are refreshed periodically. Besides that, it is highly recommended to obtain opinions of different communities when collecting the data so that any biases that the data analysts may not see can be detected. Accurate results from the AI system depend on the use of data reflecting the real world.

  Ensure a diverse range of samples in AI training sets through preprocessing methods such as data augmentation.

- **Fairness-Aware Algorithms**

  Procedures that make use of counterfactual fairness algorithms allow for decision-making to be independent of any sensitive attributes. Equitable decision-making processes are key for developing AI technologies, and fairness algorithms aid in this by allowing changes to the decision threshold depending on the attributes.

  Among the many benefits of using a fairness-based approach in machine learning, creating decision-making algorithms that are not biased, especially regarding race and gender issues, is considered key. Algorithms designed to be fair take actions on the training data prior to processing, during processing (in-processing), and even after processing of the algorithm outputs.

- **AI Audits and Ethical Guidelines**

  Documentation and explanation of models and AI decision-making processes foster transparency, instill trust, and assure responsibility. This ensures that ethical guidelines are followed and any biases are detected through regular audit and evaluation of fairness. Ethical reflection is necessary for developing and implementing trusted and accountable AI. It becomes very important to align AI technology with societal values.

  Everything will remain in control and issues generated by AI can be corrected if there are proper mechanisms of accountability in place. If ethical guidelines for AI deployment are followed and regular evaluations take place, fairness and transparency can be ensured in the application of AI.

Non-Discrimination in AI

AI has ushered in swift changes across various dimensions of societal existence, ranging from business and finance to even personal life itself. Human decisions that have a profound impact on people's lives have now been entrusted to AI in such diverse areas as diagnosis in healthcare, decision-making in finance, hiring processes, policing, and so forth. Ethical issues with these technologies are plentiful, and chief among them is the problem of non-discrimination, notwithstanding the innovations, efficiencies, and scalability they bring. It is essential that we ensure AI algorithms are unbiased and do not reinforce discrimination or widen existing inequalities for the sake of building trust and accountability in the digital world today.

AI non-discrimination means that an AI system should be able to treat everyone equally without discriminating against them on the grounds of their race, gender, age, religion, disability, socio-economic background, or any other factor. This concept is similar to human rights principles and anti-discrimination legislation present in many countries. But while it seems simple, putting it into action for AI technology becomes difficult when one considers that the AI is trained on datasets that might have biases themselves.

Bias within the data is another important source of bias within AI. To discern patterns and make predictions, machine learning algorithms require vast amounts of data. The AI system is capable of internalizing biases and inequalities embedded within the data used for its training. For example, an algorithm that aims to recruit people using the data collected while there was discrimination against some groups might result in favoring people from those particular groups when recruiting in the future. The phrase "garbage in, garbage out" is commonly employed to describe the idea.

Algorithm design is yet another major factor that contributes to AI bias. Although there is an equal representation of the data set, algorithm design might result in bias. Algorithm design is normally done in order to maximize efficiency and not equality. In other words, one population can be exposed to the effects of the AI technology or process but another might not experience anything due to the inefficiencies in the algorithm design process.

In addition to this, discrimination in artificial intelligence is important when there are stakes at play. For instance, when considering medical situations, artificial intelligence that discriminates based on factors such as demographics will offer unequal recommendations to patients. In criminal justice situations, an algorithm employed by law enforcement to detect future criminals can potentially be discriminatory against certain geographical regions. In financial systems, artificial intelligence that makes predictions regarding loan offers may not offer a loan to someone because they know someone else who was discriminated against.

In order to lessen the impact of these problems, it is crucial to adopt preventive actions to ensure the neutrality of AI technology. One of the key ways to do this is through the use of a diverse and representative dataset. Using data from various demographics helps developers mitigate bias in their development of AI technologies. It is essential to remember that using diverse data is not sufficient; the process through which the data was obtained must also be assessed.

An important tactic in this regard is the use of fairness-aware algorithms. Scientists have introduced numerous ways to evaluate and minimize the discrimination created by AI-based models, including approaches like fairness constraints, reweighting, and adversarial debiasing. These tools help in ensuring that AI algorithms create fair results for all people. Fairness cannot be achieved perfectly, however, because different types of fairness can contradict each other. Thus, while maintaining equality of accuracy among groups is possible, it will mean inequality in terms of error rates.

Transparency and explainability are just as important in ensuring non-discrimination in AI. This is because deep-learning-based AI technology functions in a manner that is often referred to as a "black box." This makes it difficult to detect any form of discrimination. Transparency is important because organizations will be able to detect and eliminate biases through the development of models that can easily be understood and the explanation of decision-making processes. Explain ability becomes more critical in sectors where there are rules about how individuals' money should be handled.

Accountability measures are as crucial as well in ensuring equality. The organizations that make use of AI technologies have to put into place effective organizational structures that incorporate ethical frameworks, auditing procedures, and supervisory boards. Independent audits may prove helpful in uncovering any existing discrimination and ensuring compliance with the standards of justice. Moreover, businesses have to ensure that individuals are able to challenge the decisions made on the basis of AI easily. It reflects the general concept of procedural justice.

The problem of discrimination through artificial intelligence has been taken care of by laws and regulations nowadays. Governments around the world have come to accept the reality that they need to regulate artificial intelligence to prevent unfavorable outcomes. The most prevalent clauses in such regulations include impact assessment, data privacy, and anti-discrimination measures. There is a particular regulation that categorizes the use of AI technology into different levels of risk and imposes stricter constraints on higher risk cases. The objective, in essence, is to ensure that such AI technologies do not lead to any form of discrimination and rather adhere to human rights.

Apart from the above considerations, there are several others, including ethics. In the case of AI-based initiatives to tackle discrimination, corporate culture is highly important. It should always be kept in mind that everyone involved in the creation of AI should understand that his actions have far-reaching implications for society. Several options may be considered here, such as including diversity in the development process, promoting collaboration among experts, conducting bias training, etc. Adherence to ethical standards may prove extremely helpful for organizations to enhance their risk management abilities.

Another significant feature of AI that is not discriminating in any way is the involvement of key stakeholders. AI systems tend to affect various categories of people, such as users, staff, customers, and the local communities. When stakeholders are involved in the process, biases and hidden side effects will be much easier to identify. To make the AI system more diverse and fairer, we might take a more participatory approach, which would involve methods like open consultation and gathering of user feedback. This problem is particularly relevant to the less fortunate minorities who are adversely affected by the AI-based decisions.

The other issue that is associated with the application of algorithms is the compromise between fairness concerns and other measurements. There are cases where an algorithm may be made fair to all parties, hence reducing the efficiency or accuracy of the algorithm. Organizations are expected to make sure that they strike a good balance between these two issues.

As the world looks into the future with regard to non-discrimination in artificial intelligence, much of it will depend on governments, the private sector, academic institutions and civil societies. Innovations and new technologies will be critical in creating effective approaches to the detection and mitigation of discrimination. However, it is equally important to develop policies and regulations that would reflect new technological developments in the field.

Also, the design of ethical AI can be highly affected by education and awareness. If we educate individuals to understand and resist bias, we can promote a more responsible and accommodating attitude towards the study and design of AI technology. This not only involves technical skills but also moral and ethical values. It is important that individuals have the capability to determine the consequences of AI and advocate for equality since AI is increasingly integrated into everyday life.

2.3 Privacy and Data Protection in AI

Personal data as big data is considered vital in the era of artificial intelligence ("AI") in order to feed the AI system training, development, and usage. Several steps in the process of operating an AI system can use personal data, such as training of the algorithm by processing big data to identify patterns, or running the AI system that might continuously process personal data to produce output. However, the huge amounts of data usage pose great threats in terms of privacy, particularly regarding data protection, transparency, and accountability. This volume of the Prism aims at exploring the connection between AI systems and personal data, particularly the application of some provisions of the Digital Personal Data Protection Act, 2023 ("DPDPA") in relation to the usage of personal data in AI systems.

Applicability of the DPDPA

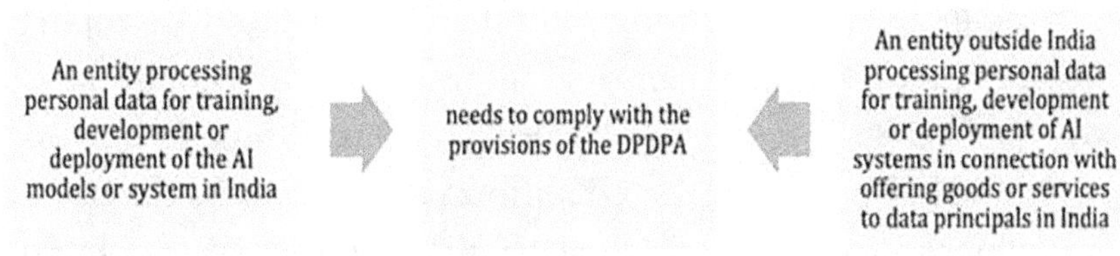

Source: (JSA, 2024)

- **Scope and Applicability of the DPDPA in AI Contexts**

  The application of DPDPA becomes difficult in cases where AI is being used internationally. For example, when non-Indian organizations use the personal information of people (data principals) residing in India for training an AI model and the final product is not sold in India, the implementation of the regulation can become problematic. The reason behind this is that under the DPDPA, the processing of personal information in a place outside India will only apply if such processing is necessary for offering goods or services to data principals living in India.

- **Publicly Available Data and AI Training**

  Another contentious issue regarding the DPDPA relates to the usage of personal data that is in the public domain. The Act makes an exception with regards to the applicability of the Act with respect to any personal data that is in the public domain either at the behest of the data principal himself/herself or through lawful means.

  This approach is far different from the international approach. For instance, the European Union's GDPR regulation covers all kinds of personal information irrespective of its being public. Moreover, there are several obligations that need to be followed for the protection of personal data. Likewise, under the Singaporean PDPA law, even if the data is public, several obligations remain.

Regulatory bodies in Europe and the UK have noted that even public information is not exempt from data protection regulations. Precautions must be taken prior to scraping this data, especially any personal information, as highlighted by the ChatGPT Taskforce of the European Data Protection Board. The same holds true for the UK Information Commissioner's Office, which puts into consideration the importance of adhering to basic data protection principles, such as a lawful basis, fairness, and transparency.

In the case of the lack of similar safeguards, invisible processing is likely to arise. It implies that people have no idea what the objective and the process of collecting their information and using it are. This opaqueness causes mistrust and ethical concerns related to the application of artificial intelligence.

Furthermore, although scraping publicly available data does not qualify as covered under the DPDPA, it can result in the violation of other regulatory instruments, including those of an intellectual property, contract law, or computer misuse law nature.

- **Anonymized Data and Regulatory Exclusion**

  The DPDPA cannot be applied to anonymized information as this information does not fall within the ambit of "personal data." Hence, an artificial intelligence model that has been developed by using an effectively anonymized dataset is also exempted from the coverage of the legislation. However, anonymization is difficult to accomplish. There is always the possibility of re-identification, particularly in cases where various datasets have been used together.

- **Legitimate Use and Purpose Limitation**

  The notion of "legitimate use" under the DPDPA establishes a valid reason for processing personal information without obtaining the consent of the concerned person under specific conditions defined by law. The cases of State operations, emergencies related to health care, purposes related to employment, and others can be considered legitimate uses under Section 7 of the Act.

Nevertheless, the use of legitimate use is restricted by the doctrine of purpose limitation. Typically, the organizations collect personal data for one purpose but later on use the same for training their AI models. According to the DPDPA, the situation needs to be re-evaluated. The fiduciaries of data should seek explicit consent for the new purposes or confirm that the processing qualifies under legitimate use.

Additionally, many AI technologies produce new personal data by profiling, inferring, or automated decision making.

- **AI in Law Enforcement and State Functions**

  Processing of personal data by the State and its agencies for the provision of services, benefits, or permits qualifies as a permissible purpose under the DPDPA and opens the floodgates for the application of AI technologies for effective administration.

  In India, many states like Tamil Nadu, Telangana, and Andhra Pradesh have deployed AI-based mechanisms for service provision in relation to water management, pension assessment, and identification of beneficiaries. Such applications illustrate how the technology can transform governance through greater efficiency and responsiveness.

  Law enforcement has also begun adopting the technology through Automated Facial Recognition Technology (AFRT) that helps to identify criminals, locate missing people, and improve the scope for surveillance. Predictive policing through the application of AI has been considered to improve efficiency in law enforcement while other AI applications have also been considered for disaster management.

There are, however, significant privacy risks associated with the deployment of these tools. The implementation of surveillance technology in public areas might result in the continuous surveillance of citizens, thereby violating their basic rights of privacy and freedom of speech. In addition to this, the DPDPA includes some exceptions to data processing in law enforcement cases, which could weaken data protection measures.

The second important problem is the existence of bias in AI algorithms. These algorithms can be biased because of their training on historical or biased data sets. Consequently, this results in the discrimination of a particular group of people based on the data fed into the AI system.

- **Processing of Personal Data of Children and Persons with Disabilities**

  The DPDPA also makes more stringent requirements regarding the processing of data belonging to children and persons with disabilities. In such situations, the data fiduciaries should seek consent of the parent or guardian of the person whose data is being processed, according to certain guidelines.

  The DPDPA also bans behavioural analysis and advertisements of children. It is noteworthy that no protection is provided in this regard for adults. This has created a loophole in the law where the issue of using AI technology involving profiling and targeted advertisements can be raised.

  Unlike the GDPR, which grants an individual the right to object or put restrictions on any processing of data involving profiling, targeted advertisements, or automated decision making, there exists a pressing need for including the principle of Responsible AI into the provisions of the DPDPA.

  Under the DPDPA, the Central Government shall have the powers to make notifications about certain categories of data fiduciaries who are exempt from seeking verifiable consent or doing behavioural monitoring and targeted advertisements in relation to children's data.

- **Research, Innovation, and Regulatory Flexibility**

  In order to foster innovations through the maintenance of an equilibrium between innovations and privacy, the provisions made under the DPDPA allow for exemptions in cases of technological development.

  Where startups are informed of an exemption granted to them by the Central Government, they will not have to go through unnecessary regulatory hoops in order to innovate or expand their business. This will prove important for the AI industry, since rapid innovation and improvements are crucial there.

  Furthermore, personal data can be processed for research, archiving, and statistics purposes, if the processing of the same personal data does not lead to decision-making on behalf of any individuals, and if it meets all the required standards.

- **Emerging Challenges and the Way Forward**

  Even though it has made significant strides in securing the data of citizens, there are still a few difficulties when it comes to the implementation of the DPDPA with AI systems. They are mainly related to regulatory issues of public domain data, inadequate regulation of cross-border activities, the dangers of secret personal data processing, and the absence of measures to prevent algorithmic biases.

  With AI becoming more common, it is necessary to consider a comprehensive regulation that links the rulings concerning data with the implementation of Responsible AI. Such measures should cover aspects such as openness equity liabilities, and empowering the individual further.

Such a harmonized regulatory framework will be indispensable for promoting innovation and maintaining trust in the era of artificial intelligence.

2.4 Accountability and Responsibility Mechanisms

These two notions are basic elements of the governance of an organization, leadership, and management. Despite the fact that the two concepts tend to be easily confused with each other, they are quite different in their nature. The processes mentioned above are important for making sure that an organization functions effectively. Therefore, it is important for modern companies to be aware of the meaning of both of these concepts.

Definition of Accountability

Accountability can be described as the responsibility one or an organization has in relation to the consequences of activities carried out. This includes being responsible for decision making, action taken, and the impact of those decisions and actions. Accountability goes further than completing assigned activities; it includes being responsible for the impact of those actions and giving an account of performance in terms of results achieved.

In organizations, accountability is normally related to positions of leadership. Those holding such positions have the responsibility to ensure goals are attained and to be accountable in case of failure, regardless of delegation of tasks.

Definition of Responsibility

Whereas responsibilities relate to the assignments, duties, or roles that are delegated to someone. This term has to do with the carrying out of certain actions and meeting the expectations of the organization or its management.

Responsibilities are usually shared and task-oriented, indicating clearly what is expected of each member of the team and how this action or activity fits into the organization's goals as a whole. This is unlike accountability since it is not a goal based but process based one.

Distinction Between Accountability and Responsibility

The difference between accountability and responsibility is an important concept to understand when designing effective organizational structures. The most pertinent differences may be outlined as the following:

- **Scope**: Accountability is broader and relates to outcomes, whereas responsibility is narrower and relates to tasks.
- **Ownership**: Responsibility is usually the domain of one person, whereas accountability can be shared by more than one member of a team.
- **Delegation**: It is possible to delegate responsibility, but accountability cannot be delegated.
- **Focus**: Accountability emphasizes results and consequences, while responsibility focuses on duties and processes.
- **Timeframe**: Accountability is often long-term and linked to strategic objectives, whereas responsibility is usually short-term and task-specific.

These distinctions highlight that while responsibilities can be transferred, accountability cannot. Even when tasks are delegated, the accountable individual remains responsible for the final outcome.

Accountability and Responsibility in Practice

For example, when we come to implementation, accountability and responsibility are correlating in a way that promoting efficiency in the enterprises.

Project manager's job comprises delegation and arranging work among members of the team. Responsibilities are processing the schedule of the tasks, dividing the work, and evaluating the team all the time. However, the accountability stays with the manager in terms of whether a project is successful or not. Failing to get the desired outcomes means explaining why it happened and making sure that it won't happen again.

So, in other words, responsibility refers to the means actions while accountability is concerned with the result.

Mechanisms for Ensuring Accountability and Responsibility

In operationalizing these means of crystal clear and transparent communication in a performance-congruent approach would Internet organizations.

1. **Clear Role Definition:** The first phase of an accountability culture should see responsibilities and roles clearly outlined. This involves job descriptions, organization charts, and RACI matrix among others to ensure that everyone knows what their role and duties are.

2. **Performance Management Systems:** Employing performance management systems such as KPIs and OKRs offers indicators to measure how well responsibility execution and accountability are being carried out. Thus, performance is kept in line with the goals of the organization, and ownership is encouraged.

3. **Governance Structures:** Committees, hierarchy of reporting, and oversight agencies are examples of governing structures that play a major role in accountability because they help monitor, analyze, and make decision-making align with organizational policies and objectives.

4. **Feedback and Evaluation Processes:** Performance appraisal and feedback mechanisms help a company evaluate the extent to which a person carries out his/her job and assumes responsibility. Such techniques like 360-degree feedback give a clear picture of his or her performance.

5. **Documentation and Reporting:** Having transparent documentation and reporting systems boosts accountability by giving an overview of the decisions, actions and results. Such mechanisms guarantee traceability and make informed decision-making.

6. **Delegation Frameworks:** An effective delegation process will make certain that delegation is done in the right way and that the right individuals are held accountable. Delegation processes help in avoiding confusion and ensure that the work is carried out effectively and that ownership is not lost.

The Interplay Between Accountability and Responsibility

Responsibility and accountability are the two terms that are closely related to each other and are complements in any corporate system. A well-developed environment of accountability can raise the efficiency of responsibility by inspiring people to do their job in an effective way.

When people understand that they have accountability to whatever occurs as a consequence of their action they feel the responsibility.

Individual and Collective Dimensions

Responsibility and accountability can be attributed to different personal and group levels.

- **Individual Responsibility**: Employees require complete knowledge of their job functions and their role in achieving company goals.

The established procedures should guide employees toward their tasks in a way that boosts productivity while preventing work duplication.

- **Collective Accountability**: Teams and organizations share responsibility for their results. Collective accountability fosters collaborative work environments which enable people to support each other while taking joint responsibility for their outcomes.

Finding a balance between these two dimensions is crucial for a harmonious, productive working environment among team members.

Role of Trust in Accountability Mechanisms

The essence of sustainable holding to account, one must build trust. Trust is a vital attribute in any setting, and in that case, individuals would be more responsible in their activities and also open to one another.

The leaders play a significant role in establishing trustful environments due to their behaviors and actions. Through being a good example and being responsible to what one does, leaders are able to build an environment where accountability is actually a strength rather than a weakness.

Common Misconceptions

Despite their importance, accountability and responsibility are often misunderstood. Some common misconceptions include:

- **Accountability equals blame**: In reality, accountability is about learning and improvement, not punishment.
- **Responsibility and accountability are identical**: While related, they serve different purposes within organizational systems.
- **Accountability is only needed in failure**: Accountability is equally important in recognizing and reinforcing success.

- **Responsibilities cannot be shared**: Responsibilities can and should be distributed to enhance collaboration.
- **Only leaders are accountable**: Accountability should exist at all levels of the organization.

It is really important to address these kinds of misconceptions to have a positive organizational culture.

Leadership and Accountability Mechanisms

Style of leadership has a significant impact on how accountability and responsibility play out.

- **Authoritarian Leadership:** Usually instills a culture of fear among its members, resulting in lack of innovation and openness.
- **Transformational Leadership:** Cultivates accountability through goal congruence and employee empowerment.
- **Servant Leadership:** Emphasizes accountability as an instrument for development and learning.

Effective leaders adapt their leadership style according to situational requirements while they maintain their authority over others and their power to grant freedom to others.

Building a Culture of Accountability

An organization can create a culture of accountability by implementing these methods:

- Specifying performance standards
- Allowing employees to make decisions
- Creating an environment of open communication
- Reinforcing accountable actions with rewards
- Continuing education and training

This approach allows accountability to be ingrained within the organization's practices without having to enforce it.

Measuring Accountability and Responsibility

To ensure effectiveness organizations need to measure and track their systems of accountability together with their systems of responsibility. The following methods can be used to achieve this objective.

- Performance metrics aligned with strategic goals
- Regular audits and compliance checks
- Employee engagement and feedback surveys
- Monitoring task completion rates and outcome quality

These measurement tools provide insights into organizational performance and highlight areas for improvement.

Benefits of Effective Mechanisms

Implementing robust accountability and responsibility mechanisms offers several benefits:

- Improved organizational performance and efficiency
- Enhanced collaboration and teamwork
- Greater transparency and trust
- Increased innovation and adaptability
- Higher employee engagement and satisfaction

These benefits contribute to the overall resilience and competitiveness of the organization.

2.5 Risk Assessment and Mitigation Strategies

In the business world today, businesses operate in an atmosphere of uncertainty and high rate of changes and therefore, they generate numerous risks that can affect them. Risk management and risk mitigation processes are after identifying and assessing these risks, facing the avenues of risk mitigation. Risk assessment is a set of activities that a company undertakes in order to calculate its vulnerability to risks and identify possible barriers to success. To mitigate implies carrying out measures to reduce the risk of occurrence of these risks.

Risk management offers a framework through which the companies prepare the troubles, improve decision making and keep operating without being interrupted. Moreover, it helps in the assurance of regulatory compliance, protection of the assets and enhancing the confidence of the stakeholders. The prioritization of the risks according to the extent of their consequences and likelihood of their occurrence will allow the clubs to spend their resources wisely and take the necessary steps.

Besides that, by adding risk assessment and planning for risk mitigation, they help to build strength and adaptability in a changing situation. No matter if it is a hospital, a bank, or a project management environment, such risk management methods result in enhanced readiness for both forecasted and unforeseen events. Hence, it is crucial to comprehend the principles of risk assessment and mitigation planning to ensure sustainable performance.

What is Risk Assessment?

As per the ISO 31000 Risk Management Standard, risk assessment is a systematic process through which organizations identify, analyze, and prioritize risks to their assets, processes, or reputation in the marketplace. As per the PwC Global Risk Survey 2024, companies that develop risk assessment methodologies and hone their skills are 50% more likely to be able to outperform their rivals in terms of financial performance. Financial institutions, for example, conduct risk assessments on a quarterly basis in order to stay compliant with regulations such as Basel III. The provision of SOC benefits such as effective risk reduction as per the risk management strategy, swift action against incidents, and continuous monitoring of threats within the cyber environment are critical for any modern-day SOC. Companies can maintain cost-effectiveness without compromising on security efficacy by conducting an evaluation of SOC as a Service Pricing Models.

What is Risk Mitigation?

"Risk mitigation" is a process through which efforts are made to minimize the risk or chances of danger occurring. One way that a MSSP can help improve this process further is by offering constant supervision of threats alongside quick response to any threat, apart from taking preventive measures that will ensure the safety of corporate activities, property, and goals from any attack. This can be achieved using the SOAR tools.

Why is Risk Assessment and Mitigation important?

Figure 2.1: Risk Assessment and Mitigation important

Source: (Rafter, 2025)

The main objective of risk assessment and mitigation is to find possible dangers, see how bad they could be, and then take the right steps to lessen their impact or chance of happening. To improve these endeavours, it is recommended to engage a managed security company. They will offer specialized knowledge and constant security monitoring.

Key objectives include:

- Protecting assets, operations, and reputation from identified risks.
- Supporting the business strategy by ensuring operational continuity.
- Prioritizing risk mitigation based on the potential impact of each risk.
- Establishing a risk management process that remains proactive and adaptive.
- Achieving an acceptable level of risk through targeted mitigation measures.

What are the steps in a risk assessment process?

Roles and duties should be clearly stated, as should asset inventories, threat sources, vulnerability analyses, possible impacts, likelihood ratings, and the plan itself. Evaluation criteria, review schedules, and data gathering procedures need to be detailed in it. Ensuring comprehensive coverage is achieved through engaging stakeholders and utilizing specialized evaluation methods. In addition, if you team up with a leading SOC provider, you may get professional analysis and real-time threat intelligence to back up your risk assessment.

An effective risk assessment framework generally follows a structured path to ensure all critical aspects of risk are covered:

- **Risk Identification:** Recognizing and listing all possible risk events that could affect operations.
- **Risk Analysis:** Assessing the level of risk by evaluating the severity and likelihood of each identified risk.
- **Risk Evaluation:** Prioritizing risks based on their potential impact on business goals and strategy.
- **Risk Mitigation Planning:** Defining appropriate measures to address high-priority risks through risk mitigation or risk transfer.
- **Implementation:** Executing the plan for mitigating the identified threats.
- **Monitoring Risk:** Continuously tracking and reviewing risk management efforts to adapt to new or evolving threats.

How do you identify and classify risks?

Risk identification is the foundation of a successful risk assessment. It involves:

- Brainstorming sessions with stakeholders to surface possible business risks.
- Reviewing historical data on past incidents and near-misses.
- Conducting interviews and surveys with subject-matter experts.
- Leveraging risk mitigation tools for automated risk detection.

Once risks are identified, classification helps in understanding the different types of risk, such as:

- Financial Risk
- Operational Risk

- Strategic Risk
- Compliance Risk
- Reputational Risk

What Are the Types of Risk Mitigation Strategies?

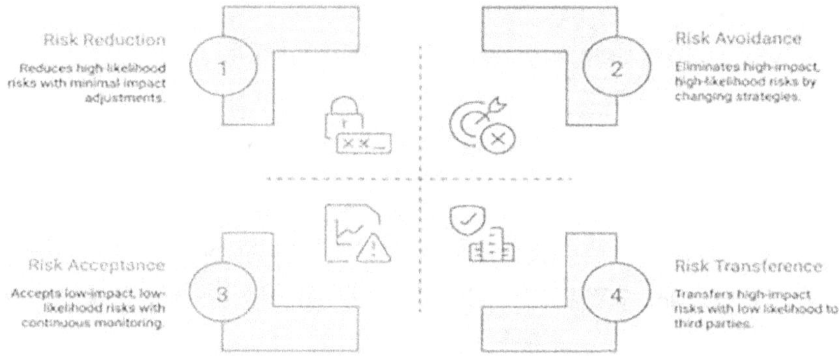

Figure 2.2: Risk Mitigation Strategies

Source: (Rafter, 2025)

In order to construct a solid risk management plan, it is crucial to comprehend risk mitigation tactics. These methods aid businesses in seeing danger, gauging its severity, and taking the necessary precautions to keep it at bay. To make sure that risk responses help businesses be more resilient, ISO 31000 states that risk management techniques should be in sync with the goals of the organization. Let's have a look at the several risk reduction measures that are now in use across various sectors.

1. **Risk avoidance**

   Risk avoidance is a proactive approach where the organization avoids the risk entirely by eliminating the activities or conditions that could cause it.

- It often involves changing business strategies, project scopes, or operational processes to steer clear of identified risks.
- By way of example, a firm may choose not to introduce a product in a market where regulatory barriers are high, and hence it will have done away with the associated risks altogether.

2. **Risk reduction**

   Risk reduction aims at reducing the probability or the possible effects of a risk. Multi-factor authentication lowers cybersecurity risks, which is implemented by 80 percent of Fortune 500 businesses.

   - It entails the application of risk controls, safety and compliance practice with the aim of minimizing the effect or degree of risk.
   - As an example, the implementation of sophisticated cybersecurity systems can minimize the effects of data breaches on the activities.

3. **Risk transference**

   Risk transference refers to the transfer of the liability of a possible risk to a third party.

   - This may be done either by outsourcing, buying insurance or by making contractual agreement that shifts the liability.
   - A common example includes buying business insurance to cover financial losses from natural disasters or supply chain disruptions.

4. **Risk acceptance**

   Risk acceptance occurs when a business consciously decides to accept the risk without taking immediate steps to mitigate it.

   - This strategy is usually chosen when the level of risk is low, the cost of mitigation is higher than the risk itself, or when mitigation is simply impractical.

   - It is crucial, however, that a risk acceptance strategy includes continuous risk monitoring to ensure that the situation does not worsen.

How do you choose the right mitigation strategy?

Choosing the best strategy requires a thorough risk assessment and a clear understanding of organizational priorities. Consider the following best practices to make informed decisions:

- Identify and analyze each risk using a qualitative risk or quantitative risk assessment framework.

- Evaluate the severity and potential impact of each risk on operations, finances, reputation, and customer trust.

- Align the choice of mitigation strategy with overall business strategy and long-term goals.

- Ensure that the risk mitigation plan is flexible enough to adjust based on changing circumstances.

- Check on the laid down plan periodically in order to make sure that it is working and any risks noted are addressed appropriately.

What Are the Best Risk Mitigation Tools and Practices?

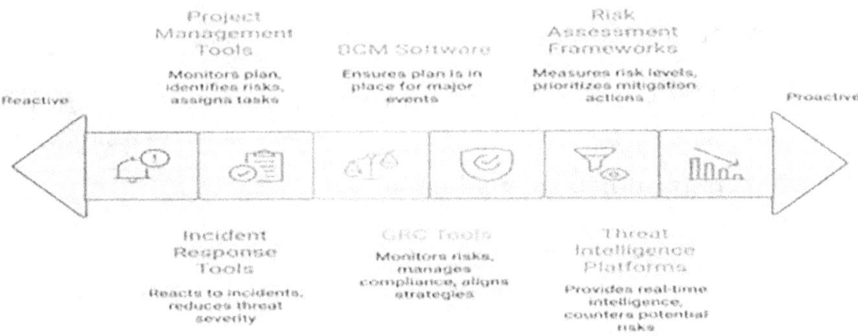

Figure 2.3: Risk Mitigation Tools and Practices

Source: (Rafter, 2025)

Risk mitigation tools and best practices are required to bring about effective risk mitigation.

The choice of the appropriate tools is a key factor in reducing the possible consequences of every risk and making sure that the risk management process is active.

Businesses today are using some of the most reliable risk mitigation tools such as:

- **Risk Assessment Frameworks:** Structured methodologies like quantitative risk assessment and qualitative risk assessment help measure risk levels and prioritize mitigation actions.
- **Business Continuity Management (BCM) Software:** Assists in ensuring a plan is in place to respond to any major risk event or disruption.
- **Threat Intelligence Platforms:** Provide real-time security intelligence for anticipating and countering potential risks before they escalate.

- **GRC Tools (Governance, Risk, and Compliance):** Help businesses monitor identified risks, manage compliance, and align risk mitigation strategies with their overall business strategy.
- **Project Management Tools:** Platforms like Asana or Monday.com support risk identification, task assignment, and monitoring the established plan across projects.
- **Incident Response and** SIEM **Tools:** Enable continuous monitoring risk activities, helping businesses detect and react to incidents, reducing the severity of potential threats.

Leading businesses use MetricStream and RSA Archer to automate governance, risk, and compliance processes (Fregly, 2025).

Multiple Choice Questions (MCQs)

1. **What is the primary component of trust in AI systems?**

   A. High computational speed

   B. Transparency and reliability

   C. Large datasets

   D. Complex algorithms

5. **AI bias typically arises due to:**

   A. Excessive computing power

   B. Poor user interfaces

   C. Biased training data

   D. Fast processing speed

5. **Which principle ensures AI treats all individuals equally?**

   A. Accountability

   B. Fairness

   C. Transparency

   D. Scalability

5. **Which technique helps protect user data in AI systems?**

   A. Data duplication

   B. Data anonymization

   C. Data inflation

   D. Data compression

5. **What is the main purpose of data protection laws in AI?**

   A. Increase AI speed

   B. Protect personal information

   C. Improve graphics

   D. Enhance storage

5. **Accountability in AI means:**

   A. AI systems operate independently

   B. Humans are responsible for AI decisions

   C. AI replaces human decisions

   D. AI systems require no monitoring

5. **Which mechanism helps trace AI decision-making processes?**

   A. Black-box models

   B. Logging and auditing

   C. Data deletion

   D. Encryption

5. **Risk assessment in AI involves:**

   A. Ignoring uncertainties

   B. Identifying potential harms

   C. Increasing model size

   D. Reducing dataset size

5. **Which is a mitigation strategy for AI risks?**

    A. Eliminating all data

    B. Regular testing and monitoring

    C. Ignoring system errors

    D. Reducing transparency

5. **Which of the following best describes a trustworthy AI system?**

    A. Fast but opaque

    B. Accurate but biased

    C. Transparent, fair, and accountable

    D. Complex and expensive

Answers

1	2	3	4	5	6	7	8	9	10
B	C	B	B	B	B	B	B	B	C

Chapter 3

Transparency and Explainability

3.1 The Need for Transparent AI Models

Transparency of artificial intelligence models means that people can understand how they operate. Transparency of AI models allows for giving explicit explanations about the processing of data and the reasoning behind conclusions reached, whereas regular black-box models provide output without explaining their reasoning process, such as complex deep learning models. The transparency of AI models is based on three key components: interpretability (which refers to understanding feature impacts), explain ability (the capacity to give reasons for decisions made), and traceability (to track how data goes through the model). The transparency of AI models is particularly relevant in cases when decisions made have implications for people's lives, meaning that they need explanations, such as medicine, banking, jurisprudence, and government-related industries. For example, bank customers can demand to know whether the reason for rejecting a loan was the person's credit rating, while professionals in medicine might be interested in knowing why an AI recommended a particular treatment method. Transparency of AI models helps increase their usability, thus enhancing trust in AI models, making them accountable due to the possibility of tracking decisions, and avoiding any biases that lead to unequal outcomes. Legal and regulatory frameworks require that enterprises should explain how automated judgments are given; transparent AI assists in this. The first is to adopt models that are simple to comprehend and interpret by themselves, such as decision trees and linear regression; the second is to adopt techniques such as LIME and SHAP to clarify complex models once they have already been utilized to make predictions; the last is the objective of gaining transparency with both of these approaches. Although transparent AI has many advantages, it also has some drawbacks, such as the fact that very accurate models tend to be more complicated and harder to understand and explain. Explaining things can sometimes cause people to worry about their privacy, and it can be hard to provide transparency in large-scale systems. However, in order to promote justice, responsibility, and ethical technology usage, transparent AI is an essential part of ethical AI. An key feature for constructing dependable, trustworthy, and human-centered AI systems, transparency will be in high demand as AI evolves and becomes more integrated into everyday life (Meyes, 2022).

Why is AI transparency important?

On a daily basis, tens of millions of individuals across the globe use artificial intelligence applications like recommendation engines, virtual agents, and generative AI chatbots. Users may only stand to lose time or money if the model turns out to be biased or incorrect, thus there's probably no need to be transparent about how these AI tools function for low-stakes decision-making.

The use of artificial intelligence (AI) technologies to guide critical decisions is, however, expanding across industries. Investment decisions, medical diagnosis, hiring decisions, criminal sentences, and many more tasks are now assisted by AI. Potentially considerably more harmful outcomes could result from biased or incorrect AI outputs in certain instances. A person's life savings, professional prospects, or even years of their life can be lost in an instant.

In order for stakeholders to trust AI's decision-making capabilities, it is essential to be able to see how the models are built, the logic behind the algorithms, and how the model's accuracy and fairness are evaluated. The first thing they need to understand are data sources and processes-how to weight both model training and labeling tuning.

Transparency in AI not only helps to establish trust, but it also encourages collaboration and the sharing of knowledge within the AI ecosystem, which ultimately leads to better AI. Organizations can put less emphasis on worrying about the reliability of AI and more on utilizing AI technologies to accomplish business goals if they are transparent by default.

AI transparency regulations and frameworks

There is a complex web of regulations that govern AI use, and it is always changing. Meeting the needs of model validators, auditors, and regulators—as well as complying with these regulations—requires transparent model processes. The European Union's Artificial Intelligence Act was the first of its kind in the world.

1. **The EU AI Act**

   The European Union's (EU) Artificial Intelligence Act uses a risk-based approach to regulation, classifying AI regulations according to the danger they represent. It bans some AI usage outright and requires others to adhere to stringent standards of openness, risk management, and governance. Certain forms of AI are subject to extra disclosure requirements. To illustrate:

   - AI systems that are meant to have direct conversations with humans should be made to disclose that they are talking to an AI system, unless it's clear from the context. For instance, a chatbot ought to be made to reveal its identity to users.

   - In order to identify their outputs as being generated or altered by AI, systems that generate text, graphics, or specific other types of information must adopt machine-readable formats. Deepfakes, created by AI, are manipulated photos or videos that pretend to depict someone doing or saying something they didn't actually do or say.

Several nations have passed laws protecting citizens' private information in response to the EU's General Data Protection Regulation (GDPR). In a similar vein, industry watchers believe the EU AI Act will encourage the creation of global AI ethics and compliance guidelines.

What is model transparency and how does it relate to Explainable AI?

A machine learning model is considered transparent if its structure and decision-making process are easy to understand and comprehend. Data scientists, developers, and end-users are all part of the stakeholders who need to be able to access and understand the model's structure, parameters, and decision routes. A transparent model makes it easier to understand both the algorithm and the data that go into predicting certain things. Since it gives a glimpse of why a machine learning model predicts something or does something, it is essential for ensuring trust and accountability.

Model transparency is an idea that is very much connected to XAI or explainable artificial intelligence. The machine learning algorithms need to produce results which human users can both comprehend and trust. The purpose of transparency is to show how a specific model function. The process of explain ability enables users to understand the reasons which drive model decisions.

Explainable artificial intelligence (AI) requires model transparency because it serves as the fundamental element for creating human-understandable explanations. Transparent model structures enable developers to create understandable explanations more efficiently because they gain access to both the model's decision-making processes and the key elements that drive its performance.

The concepts become more important because they apply to healthcare and banking and legal affairs, which need AI decisions to be understood because of their significant impact. Fair and ethical AI in various fields requires that all parties comprehend the process through which the AI models arrive at their conclusions. Many regions require enterprises to establish AI systems which guarantee both fairness and accountability.

The methods for analyzing the importance of the features allow us to find out the factors influencing the output of the model because it allows building the model that we can interpret. The second approach employs visual analysis to explain how the decision tree boundary works and how the output of the model is influenced by various input values.

Nevertheless, what should be highlighted too is that the confidence and trust in the use of AI will also be enhanced because of the transparency of models and Explainable AI. Both aspects are equally critical for proper and ethical utilization of AI due to their ability to explain AI actions.

Importance of Transparent AI Models

- **Building Trust:** One of the key benefits of open AI systems is establishing trust. When people can comprehend the rationale behind decisions made by the AI system, they are much more likely to trust the system. For instance, in a situation involving diagnostic services, a doctor must be able to understand the rationale behind an AI's recommended treatment.
- **Accountability:** It is easier for stakeholders to monitor the decision-making process through transparency. This is even more important when handling issues that have greater significance such as in the case of the criminal justice system and the loan business.
- **Bias Detection and Fairness:** When using open models, bias detection is easier to detect whether in the training data or in the process of making decisions. This way, we reduce chances of bias and ensure fairness.
- **Regulatory Compliance:** The demand for transparency from AI is increasing with each passing day. This is because data protection

regulations, among others, require firms to explain automated decisions.

- **Improved Decision-Making:** Transparent AI systems provide feedback on their outputs for users and thus help to better educate the users about what to expect. Such improved education helps in making decisions that could lead to better outcomes.

Explainable AI (XAI): Methods and Tools

The term "explainable artificial intelligence" (XAI) describes a set of practices that make it possible for machine learning algorithms to provide trustworthy, comprehensible results for humans to interpret. When people talk about deep learning, they often bring up explainable AI, which is an important part of the FAT machine learning paradigm. With XAI, businesses can build trust before implementing AI. With the help of XAI, they can better comprehend the actions of an AI model and spot issues before they happen. In the end, explainable AI is useful because it can provide trustworthy machine-learning models that are clear and easy to interpret. This value has the potential to bring about numerous benefits across various areas and applications.

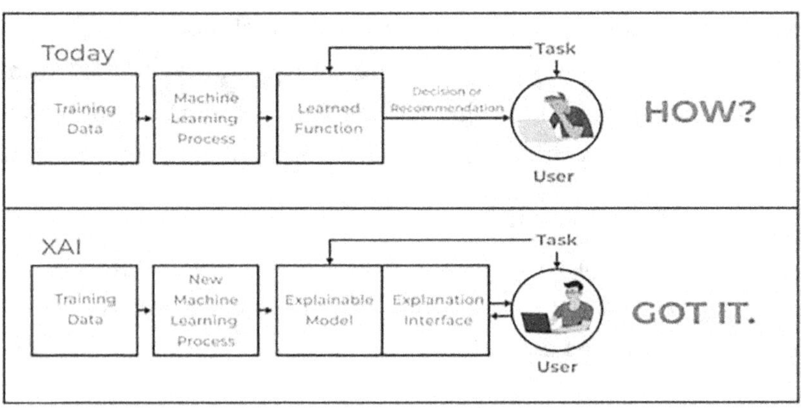

Figure 3.1: Explainable Artificial Intelligence Concept

Source: (Geeksforgeeks, 2026)

Benefits of explainable AI

Machine learning models that are both transparent and interpretable are valuable because they allow humans to understand and trust them. This is where explainable AI comes in. This value has the potential to bring about numerous benefits across various areas and applications. Here are a few important benefits of explainable AI:

1. **Improved decision-making:** With the help of explainable AI, it is possible to gain useful insights and knowledge that can enhance decision-making. If we want to know what aspects are most important for the model's predictions, explainable AI can help us out with that.

2. **Increased trust and acceptance:** Explainable artificial intelligence improves public confidence in machine learning models by solving the problems which exist in outdated machine learning systems that lack transparency.

3. **Reduced risks and liabilities:** Explainable AI provides organizations with a framework which helps them meet their ethical requirements and their regulatory obligations regarding machine learning systems. the research shows that decreased liability and risk from machine learning systems create multiple advantages which benefit different fields and their respective use cases.

How does Explainable AI work?

The techniques and approaches used to make machine learning models transparent and interpretable determine the architecture of explainable AI. But generally speaking, there are three main parts to explainable AI architecture:

- **Machine learning model:** This model stands for the underlying algorithms and processes that produce predictions and inferences from data; it is the central component of explainable AI. This part can be built using many different machine learning algorithms, including supervised, unsupervised, and reinforcement learning. It has several potential uses in fields like computer vision, medical imaging, and natural language processing.

- **Explanation algorithm:** This part of explainable AI helps to identify the most important and significant aspects in the model's predictions by analyzing and providing information about those factors. This part can shed light on how the ML model functions and can be based on various explainable AI techniques including feature importance, attribution, and visualization.
- **Interface:** The explainable AI interface is what shows humans the data and insights that the explanation algorithm has developed. This part of the explainable AI system can be built on top of a variety of technologies and platforms, including web apps, mobile apps, and visualizations, and it can give a natural and easy way for users to access and work with the data and insights it generates.

Explainable AI principles

In order to create and release machine learning models that are both visible and interpretable, a set of concepts called explainable AI (XAI) can be utilized.

- **Transparency:** XAI should be forthright about what it does and why it does it, including providing details on which factors have the most impact on the model's predictions. By being open and honest, XAI can gain trust and acceptance, which in turn can lead to useful insights and advantages across many domains and applications.
- **Interpretability:** XAI should offer a straightforward and easy-to-understand method for understanding and utilizing the insights and

data it generates. This interpretability has the potential to deliver useful insights and advantages across domains and applications, while also helping to overcome the constraints and difficulties of conventional machine learning models.

- **Accountability:** In order to address the ethical and regulatory concerns surrounding machine learning, XAI needs to take responsibility and lay forth a plan. the ethical and accountable use of XAI, which has the potential to yield important insights and advantages across various domains and applications, can be enhanced by this accountability.

Explainable AI approaches

The goal of various explainable AI methods is to create machine learning models that are easier to understand and work with. Here are a few examples of popular explainable AI methods:

- **Feature importance:** This method assumes that various input features or variables have varied but complementary contributions to the model's predictions. The feature importance techniques identify which features produce accurate predictions by ranking them from their highest to lowest levels of importance.
- **Attribution:** This technique works under the presumption that all features or variables used in the modeling process have their unique and quantified influence on the predictions made by the model. The aim of the attribution techniques is to allocate the predictions made by the model to the individual features used for training.
- **Visualization:** The approach is based on the idea that unlike numbers and texts, visuals and graphics for machine learning models might provide better insights. Thus, by developing an interactive graphical view of the model architecture, parameters, and outputs, it is expected that we gain insight into its performance and behavior.

3.2 Explainable AI (XAI) Techniques

To implement explainable AI (XAI) in python, you can use one of the following approaches:

- **LIME (Local Interpretable Model-agnostic Explanations):** The widely-used approach in XAI relies on local modeling to reveal the factors that have the greatest impact on the predictions made by the model. The python lime library facilitates the use of LIME with its numerous functions and features.
- **SHAP (SHapley Additive exPlanations):** This XAI method takes a page out of game theory's Shapley value and applies it to XAI; it then gives us insights into what matters most for the model's predictions and we can understand and explain them. The shap package provides users with tools and functions which they can use to create and interpret SHAP explanations; this package serves as an effective method to implement SHAP in Python programming language.
- **ELI5 (Explain Like I'm 5):** This XAI method uses straightforward, easy-to-understand language that even non-experts can understand to reveal which elements have the most impact on the model's predictions. You can utilize the eli5 package in Python to implement ELI5. It offers many tools and functions for creating and understanding ELI5 explanations.

A number of methods exist for implementing XAI in Python, such as LIME, SHAP, and ELI5. With their varied degrees of interpretability and explainability, these methods find usage in many diverse contexts.

3.3 Documentation, Reporting, and Model Cards

Transparency, accountability, and responsibility are among the most important issues in the rapidly growing realm of artificial intelligence (AI). Considering the application of AI algorithms in such spheres as health care, financial sector, education, recruitment, and even governmental institutions, the problem of the way AI algorithms work, the process of decision-making, and its risks cannot be disregarded any longer. The growing need for transparency and clarity in regard to the operation of artificial intelligence algorithms led to the development of such systematic approaches as documentation, reporting, and model cards. Note that all three methods are critical for interpreting and explaining your AI systems.

The documentation describes each of the processes of an AI system, which includes all the processes of data collection until the deployment of the system. The reporting process is meant to provide information on system performance along with the risks and impacts of the system in an easy-to-understand format. Model cards provide the entire picture of a model as they display its key characteristics that comprise its purpose of use and its limitations. All of this together amounts to the basic structure that can provide for the ethical evolution or oversight of artificial life systems.

Documentation in AI

AI system transparency depends on documentation which serves as its fundamental element. The process requires documentation of every pertinent detail related to the model's complete development lifecycle from its design to its actual deployment. The AI systems achieve their three critical qualities of understanding, reproducibility, and auditing through proper documentation practices.

- **Importance of Documentation**

  The main function of documentation exists to support reproducibility efforts. Scientific and technical disciplines require reproducibility because it provides the means to authenticate findings and test their authentication. The AI development process requires researchers and developers to create documentation which shows all development activities to enable model replication and performance validation.

The documentation system establishes responsibility for all actions. The ability to trace AI system decision-making back to its initial development point becomes necessary when those decisions lead to major outcomes. The development process documentation maintains a complete record which shows all development decisions including data selection and model development and parameter adjustment activities.

The main use of documentation has been to expose bias and mistakes.AI models function according to their training data which means that any biases within that data will result in the model generating discriminatory results. The documentation process helps developers to identify potential bias sources which they need to address through active solutions.

The documentation process enables different teams to work together. The AI project needs involvement from data scientists and engineers and domain specialists and government officials. The documentation system provides all project participants with a unified understanding of the system through its organized and comprehensive presentation.

Key Components of Documentation

Effective AI documentation typically includes several key components:

- **Data Documentation**: This includes information about the sources of data, methods of data collection, preprocessing steps, and any known biases or limitations.
- **Model Architecture**: A detailed description of the algorithms and structures used in the model, such as neural networks, decision trees, or ensemble methods.
- **Training Procedure:** Details regarding the process of training the model, such as hyperparameters used, techniques used for optimization, and training time.

- **Performance Metrics:** Description of the methods of measuring the performance of the model, including accuracy, precision, recall, and F1 score.
- **Risks and Limitations:** Possible limitations, risks, and conditions where the model can fail.
- **Deployment:** Information regarding deployment and the interaction of the model with end-users.

Challenges in Documentation

Organizations need essential documentation for their operations, but they struggle to create effective documentation. The organization needs to document its AI system completely, but its complex nature prevents all essential elements from being documented. Continuous effort is required to keep the documentation up-to-date since it involves model upgrades and needs more documentation.

- **Reporting in AI**

  The documentation function expects its employees to record comprehensive technical information. The objective of AI reporting is to assist in understanding the performance of the system and any associated risks that may arise from them.

- **Purpose of Reporting**

  The main purpose of AI reporting exists to create transparency which enables people to make educated choices. The reports present technical information through accessible formats which business leaders and regulators and end-users can understand.

  Organizations need to use reporting for their requirements to comply with regulations. Companies must provide evidence that they have met the criteria for fairness, reliability, and accountability through various laws and regulations. These reports provide evidence that companies need to meet these requirements.

Reporting also plays another important role in risk management. Safety procedures of AI systems deployment are developed by organizations through the evaluation of possible risks alongside their effect.

Types of AI Reports

There are several types of reports commonly used in AI:

- **Performance Reports**: These summarize the model's performance using metrics such as accuracy, precision, recall, and F1-score. Comparisons between data sets may also be part of these assessments.
- **Reports on Fairness and Bias:** The fairness and bias reports help to determine whether the model discriminates against certain groups.
- **Risk Assessment Reports:** This report highlights risks that may come up from the AI model.
- **Audit Reports:** These are independent evaluations done on the AI system.
- **Impact Assessment Report:** This examines the consequences that the AI system will have on society at large.

Best Practices in Reporting

Effective reporting requires three main requirements that entail transparent presentation and accurate contents and relevant information. The report needs to match the requirements of its intended audience which requires making technical information more understandable to people without expertise. Visual aids such as charts, graphs, and dashboards enable better communication of complex information than people can understand through words.

Reports should be periodically updated that reflects improvement of models and changes in its running conditions. The stakeholders need to know the limitations of the system that incorporate all uncertainties as they will enable them to have the right expectations on the system performance.

Model Cards

Model cards are a comparatively new technology in AI transparency. They allow the standardization of summarizing essential information regarding machine learning models in a simple and clear manner.

What Are Model Cards?

The model card is a paper that comes with a trained AI model and contains the necessary information concerning its purpose, performance, and limitations. It is formulated in a way that is easily comprehended by a broad group of stakeholders such as developers, policymakers and end-users.

Benefits of Model Cards

Model cards help the user to comprehend the potential and constraints of AI systems easier. They assist in avoiding misuse through clearly defining what should and should not be used. Through their emphasis on possible biases and ethical issues, model cards will help developers to resolve them and bring fairness to the game.

Integration of Documentation, Reporting, and Model Cards

Even though documentation, reporting, and model cards are of different purpose, they are highly intertwined. Documentation gives the technical background, reporting gives the important insights to the stakeholders and the model cards give a succinct summary to be referred to at a glance.

These combined practices form an overall framework for transparency that promotes the responsible creation of AI technology. They enable the companies to win the confidence of the users and also to assure the regulatory compliance and ethical use of the technology.

Challenges and Limitations

There is nothing problematic with the introduction of effective documentation, reporting, and model cards. Lack of standardization is one of the biggest problems as it may create inconsistency and confusion. The second issue is that the practices are resource-intensive since they require time, expertise and constant maintenance.

It is also not easy to balance transparency and intellectual property issues and privacy. It is imperative that organizations should make sure that they offer enough information without revealing sensitive information or secret algorithms.

Future Trends

It is possible that AI transparency in the future will be more standardized and automated. New tools are being developed to automatically create documentation and reports, limiting the work load of developers. The regulatory structures are also becoming stricter and the organizations are expected to be open in their operations.

It is believed that model cards will become more interactive and dynamic where users will be able to explore model behavior in real time. Also, fairness and ethical considerations will be given more focus, which is influenced by increasing the role of responsible AI.

3.4 Auditing and Independent Oversight

When applied to artificial intelligence (AI), auditing and independent oversight are fundamentally the procedures and devices that aid us verify up, monitor, and ensure that AI frameworks perform reasonably in an accountable manner, and according to the regulations. That is the right step to take, otherwise it is difficult to trust AI systems, particularly when they get involved in such a critical issue as healthcare finance governance and even law enforcement.

Audits in AI entail detailed and systematic examination and evaluation of design, data, algorithms, and outcomes associated with the AI system. The goal of conducting an audit in AI is to ensure that the system runs as specified and fulfills the ethical, legal, and performance criteria. AI audits may be conducted by either the company or an independent third party. Typically, audits are carried out to examine the accuracy, consistency, fairness, quality of data, bias, compliance with laws, and security. For instance, an audit may seek to uncover whether there is discrimination against certain groups in hiring through an automated system or whether a credit scoring model provides accurate and unbiased results.

There exist several forms of AI audits. Some of them include technical audits that concentrate mainly on the performance of the AI models, and the ethical audit that assesses matters concerning social impacts, fairness, and biases in the AI system. Audits are useful to the firms as they identify areas of concern and make corrective measures in order to improve the AI systems.

Independent Oversight refers to the external and objective individuals or agencies that supervise and control the AI system to ensure its proper utilization. Some examples of independent oversight include government agencies, regulatory bodies, independent review committees, and third parties. The primary purpose of independent oversight is to provide an impartial assessment of the AI systems without any conflict of interests from the organizational standpoint.

Independent oversight is simply a valuable source of responsibility since it ensures that organizations need to explain the outcomes of their AI systems. Moreover, it is the means of applying ethical standards, protecting user rights, and adhering to the law. As an example, the regulatory bodies can make it a requirement that organizations submit their AIs to be evaluated before the launching or they can regulate the post-deployment monitoring to check on the consistent compliance.

In case of auditing along with independent oversight, it is an essential part of AI governance. On the one hand, the auditing reaches the bottom of the functioning of the system within, on the other hand, there is an independent control that these observations are not only unbiased, but also most suited to the needs of society and regulators in general. Despite the fact that these two aspects cannot be separated the implementation has several challenges including the absence of universal auditing processes, technical issues and shortage of professional manpower make the process difficult.

Types of AI Audits

1. **Technical Audits:** The main objective of technical audits is to evaluate the performance and effectiveness of the AI system. This includes evaluating parameters such as accuracy rate of the model, robustness of the model, scalability of the model, and data quality used in the system. Other than that, technical audits are used to test whether the model offers consistent results in varying circumstances.

2. **Ethical Audits:** They verify whether AI system is not discriminative, fair, and does not violate human rights among other ethics. The purpose is to find prejudices in data or algorithms, which might result in the different treatment of individuals or groups.

3. **Compliance Audits:** Compliance audits confirm the compliance of the AI system to the existing laws, rules, and other standards in the industry. This type of audit is necessary when the business is controlled, such as finance and healthcare.

4. **Operational Audits:** Operational audits determine the use of the AI system in the real-life settings. They evaluate workflows,

human interaction, and system integration to ensure effective and responsible deployment.

5. **Security Audits:** A security audit is conducted on the AI system to find out the weaknesses that can be exploited for any malicious intention by some individuals. Moreover, the audits help evaluate the data and cyber security threats.

Key Components of AI Auditing

- **Data Assessment:** The primary ingredient for the success of an AI algorithm is good data. The auditing process entails evaluating the data sources, their quality and representativeness as well as identifying any forms of bias present.
- **Model Evaluation:** The auditor evaluates the architecture of the model together with the underlying parameters and algorithms used and makes sure that they are appropriate for the job. This process entails testing the model using different conditions.
- **Performance Metrics:** Some of the commonly used metrics in evaluating AI algorithms include accuracy, precision, recall and the F1 score among others. An auditor makes sure that these metrics are appropriate.
- **Evaluation of Fairness and Bias:** In auditing, the model is assessed regarding its ability to generate equitable outputs with respect to different demographics. It facilitates identification of any forms of discrimination.
- **Transparency and Explainability:** In auditing, an AI algorithm is assessed on the basis of its explainability. A transparent algorithm makes it easy to audit.
- **Document Assessment:** A comprehensive documentation plays a major role during auditing. Auditors review the relevant documents concerning the data, model building and implementation processes.

Importance of AI Auditing

The existing need to audit AI is fraught by a large number of factors that require its actual implementation to prevent this dire situation. The first benefit of trust in AI systems occurs when organizations demonstrate their systems deliver trustworthy performance. The second benefit enables organizations to find and correct their security risks before any harm occurs. The first benefit of auditing enables organizations to show they comply with rules and regulations while decreasing their chances of facing legal problems. The present system status determines the performance of the organization based on compliance auditing procedures to identify operational areas which can be improved.

Independent Oversight in AI

The notion of independent oversight will involve the involvement of third-party agencies in the regulation and administration of AI technologies. Such agencies could be government bodies, police forces, independent auditors, educational bodies, or even communities.

Purpose of Independent Oversight

Autonomous regulation, on the other hand, intends to ensure that AI systems are applied in a proper way and for the good of all members of the society. The independent review ensures that there is an unbiased examination of the AI system without any personal or financial interests involved.

Key Functions of Independent Oversight

- Monitoring compliance with laws and regulations
- Evaluating ethical implications of AI systems
- Ensuring accountability for AI-driven decisions

- Protecting user rights and privacy
- Promoting transparency and public trust

Forms of Independent Oversight

- **Regulatory Oversight:** The government agencies introduce regulations and guidelines to AI development and deployment. They can make organizations audit, report, or seek approvals before the implementation of AI systems.
- **Third-Party Audits:** Independent organizations conduct audits to evaluate AI systems. These audits provide an unbiased assessment of performance and compliance.
- **Ethics Committees and Review Boards:** Organizations may establish independent ethics committees to review AI projects and ensure they align with ethical principles.
- **Public and Civil Society Oversight:** The Non-governmental organizations and advocacy groups contribute to the monitoring of AI systems and creating concerns regarding possible risks.

Benefits of Independent Oversight

The independent oversight improves the accountability of the organization because the organization is now responsible for its artificial intelligence. Oversight ensures that the decision-making process is unbiased and promotes adherence to ethical principles. Moreover, oversight identifies risks and prevents damage, which makes individuals and society safe. Finally, oversight helps build trust by proving that artificial intelligence can be externally examined.

Relationship Between Auditing and Independent Oversight

There exists an extremely close connection between auditing and independent oversight. These two activities are perfectly compatible, and when combined, they create an excellent foundation for the governance of artificial intelligence. On the one hand, auditing provides an extremely thorough examination of the AI system. On the other hand, independent oversight ensures that such an examination is both objective and takes into consideration the expectations of society as a whole.

The organization, for example, can carry out its own internal audit to evaluate how well the model performs. On the other hand, the external regulator reviews the outcome of the assessment to ensure that there is no violation of any law or ethical principles.

3.5 Communicating AI Decisions to Stakeholders

Communicating AI decision-making to stakeholders basically entails the process of explaining the logic or reasoning involved in making decisions by the AI, or any prediction or recommendation provided by the AI. Normally, stakeholders could be the developer, management, regulator, customer, employees, and anyone else influenced by the decisions made by AI. In light of the fact that AI technology has been adopted into processes that affect people's lives, for instance, the medical field, finance, recruitment, or even government affairs, the ability to make clear and explain those decisions made by the AI has now become a necessity. Effective communication will help the stakeholders trust the AI, understand its decision-making, and make decisions based on the outputs.

In essence, when it comes to explaining decisions made by AI, it involves translating very complex technical elements into understandable information. AI models, particularly complex ones like machine learning and deep learning, are likely to act as black boxes in that it becomes extremely challenging, even impossible, to comprehend how it makes decisions to non-technical users. Hence, one should have the necessity to bridge this gap by providing adequate explanations that would apply to various audiences. As an example, a data scientist may expect to be provided with a highly technical description of how the model and algorithms perform, but a customer may only need to be told why he/she is/is not being approved or denied a loan.

Another significant dimension that should be discussed in terms of explaining the decisions of AI systems is explanation of ability. It is concerned with making the justification of a particular outcome of a model in an easily comprehensible manner. Such tools as feature importance, visualization and a short commentary can serve excellently as teaching content that can be used to provide the meaning of the input features. As an example, an artificial intelligence algorithm applied in credit scoring can provide the answer that the loan application was denied due to such reasons as low income, colossal debts, and bad credit history.

Simplicity is another consideration to be made. The communication should not use complicated language but rather focus on talking to people in a manner that makes it easy for them to understand. Besides this, simplified complex information can be done through the use of other tools such as charts, graphs, dashboards, and heat maps.

Another essential element of the communications strategy of the AI decision-making is accountability. Everyone involved should be aware of the person that holds the AI systems and what can be done to dispute or check the ruling. The ability to present documentation in a clear way, clear record of the decision-making process, and contacts where any questions can be directed helps in creating accountability and a sense of trust.

The organization needs to investigate the ethical dimension of its problem because it requires assessment of three components which include fairness and bias and potential risks. The organization should establish procedures which guarantee that all stakeholders receive proper understanding of the AI algorithm's limitations and its uncertain results.

Different stakeholders require different communication approaches. For example:

- Technical stakeholders (developers, engineers) need detailed reports, model metrics, and algorithmic explanations.
- Business stakeholders (managers, executives) require summaries of performance, risks, and business impact.
- Regulators need compliance reports, audit results, and evidence of fairness.
- End-users or customers need simple, clear explanations of decisions affecting them.

Though it's a really crucial aspect, communicating AI decision-making does have certain problems. The model's complexity together with the need to protect intellectual property rights and the need for simplified explanations creates two different challenges which are currently unmanageable.

Multiple Choice Questions (MCQs)

1. **Why is transparency important in AI systems?**
   - A. To increase computational speed
   - B. To ensure fairness and trust in decision-making
   - C. To reduce data storage requirements
   - D. To eliminate human involvement
2. **Transparent AI models help users to:**
   - A. Ignore model outputs
   - B. Understand how decisions are made
   - C. Increase algorithm complexity
   - D. Replace all human decisions
3. **Which of the following best describes Explainable AI (XAI)?**
   - A. AI that works without data
   - B. AI systems that provide clear reasoning behind their outputs
   - C. AI used only in research labs
   - D. AI that replaces human intelligence
4. **Which method is commonly used in XAI to interpret model predictions?**
   - A. Data encryption
   - B. LIME (Local Interpretable Model-Agnostic Explanations)
   - C. Cloud storage
   - D. Data compression

5. **What is the purpose of SHAP (SHapley Additive exPlanations)?**
   A. To train deep learning models
   B. To visualize data storage
   C. To explain the contribution of each feature in a prediction
   D. To encrypt datasets
6. **What are model cards used for in AI systems?**
   A. Storing datasets
   B. Providing standardized documentation about model performance and limitations
   C. Running algorithms
   D. Increasing model accuracy
7. **Which of the following is included in a model card?**
   A. Model architecture details
   B. Intended use and limitations
   C. Performance metrics
   D. All of the above
8. **What is the main goal of AI auditing?**
   A. To improve hardware efficiency
   B. To ensure compliance, fairness, and accountability
   C. To increase model size
   D. To eliminate data preprocessing

9. **Independent oversight in AI systems helps to:**

   A. Reduce transparency

   B. Avoid accountability

   C. Provide unbiased evaluation of AI systems

   D. Eliminate regulation

10. **Why is it important to communicate AI decisions to stakeholders?**

   A. To confuse users

   B. To build trust and enable informed decision-making

   C. To hide model limitations

   D. To reduce operational costs

Answers

1	2	3	4	5	6	7	8	9	10
B	B	B	B	C	B	D	B	C	B

Chapter 4

Compliance, Regulation, and Legal Considerations

4.1 Overview of Global AI Regulations

The global framework of artificial intelligence (AI) rules is currently in the process of rapid growth due to the interaction of numerous goals of innovation and pressing risk management demands with the various regulatory strategies. The period from 2020 to 2026 was the time when the world underwent a transition from discussing regulation theoretically to establishing legal frameworks and formal regulatory systems. The process is there due to the fact that now people are aware that AI is a disruptive technology that is associated with economic gains but poses some risks in terms of its application.

There is a lot of diversity when it comes to the maturity level of regulations among different continents; however, one thing that can be noted with certainty is that wherever there was an emphasis on adopting a more strategic approach at first, there is already a drive toward adopting more legislative regulations. The example that needs to be cited here is the European Union, which was the first to adopt the famous Al Act, thus establishing standards for a risk-based approach to regulation.

The commonality between these approaches seems to stem from the full devotion towards a human-oriented approach to the governance of Al. One can see that a human-oriented approach emphasizes how AI technology must be designed in a way that will remain within human control, respect human rights, uphold principles of equality and transparency, and operate as mere helpers for humanity. One of the most important approaches where the human-oriented devotion has been manifested is the national Al strategy.

It is, after all, the governments across the globe that are leading this wave by investing heavily in their respective country's Al systems, developing talents, and promoting research and development activities. At the same time, it is important to remember that this zeal should be matched by the understanding that an unchecked innovation can be harmful too. As such, the discussion on regulations focuses on maintaining a proper balance between cultivating a thriving ecosystem for Al and staying technologically ahead by setting up appropriate barriers.

This is the reason why the environment for regulation in the international domain represents an ever-changing mosaic comprising common aspirations towards progress, differing beliefs and cultures, competing geopolitical interests, and the universal necessity to solve any challenges presented by Al. It can be noted from this that constant attempts are being made to tap into the possibilities of Al despite its dangers through Al governance in society (Calvert, 2020).

Dominant Global Trends

The global Al regulatory landscape shows three main trends that emerge across multiple regions because nations share identical regulatory challenges and collective goals, and they have developed standard practices for AI regulation.

- **Risk-Based Approaches:**

  This might even be regarded as one of the most prevalent trends across the globe. One way of classifying AI based on the degree of risk associated with it has been gaining prominence around the world, with many countries having adopted the classification guidelines contained in the EU's Al Act for the formulation of their laws. This includes the allocation of risks to categories such as "unacceptable," "high," "limited," and "minimal" risks, after which responsibility allocations will be made. Some of the high-risk industries regulated under this law include critical infrastructure, health care, law enforcement, biometric identification, and credit scoring. Regulations for these sectors involve impact assessments, obligations to disclose information, human oversight, and strict compliance assessments.

- **Human-Centricity and Ethical Principles:**

  A basic concern about humanity and ethically driven AI is an essential part of almost all forms of regulation. At the same time, principles such as transparency, responsibility, fairness, non-discrimination, privacy by design, and human oversight are of high regard. Thus, we can be sure that AI will be developed and applied in such a way that it will support human competencies, protect fundamental rights, and comply with societal values. Such principles are commonly enshrined within international organizations, state strategies, and new regulations, as there is a need to develop "trustworthy AI"

- **Data Protection as a Foundational Layer:**

  Existing or recently passed comprehensive laws governing the use of personal data are an essential horizontal foundation for AI regulation in almost any area. For example, GDPR-compliant laws (in Europe, Central & South America, Asia, MENA, and Sub-Saharan Africa) establish certain basic requirements in relation to AI systems when it comes to data processing, consent, and automated decision-making. Increasingly, national authorities for the protection of data assume jurisdiction over AI systems using personal data, creating an important means of enforcing the regulation even in the absence of separate laws addressing AI.

- **Promotion of Innovation and Al Ecosystems:**

  Even with such emphasis on regulation, there remains an overarching aim to develop thriving ecosystems of Al and ensure continued technological advancement. The governments have made substantial efforts toward Al R&D, constructing compute capabilities in the nation, nurturing Al talent, and supporting startup firms via various means. Sandboxes that provide for experimental use of innovative Al technologies under the watchful eye of relevant parties have become popular in recent years. This phenomenon is common in MENA, Sub-Saharan Africa, and even parts of Asia and Europe.

- **National Security and Digital/Al Sovereignty:**

  The increasing trend, especially visible in Asia, MENA, and increasingly in the EU and parts of Latin and Central America, relates to national security and Al sovereignty. The concept implies investments in domestic AI capacity, creating a national large language model (LLM) which incorporates local culture and language, and ensuring that there are demands regarding the localization of data. The objective is to achieve self-sufficiency and avoid dependence on foreign technologies. In North America, the same trend is visible but through slightly differing channels.

- **Shift from Soft Law to Hard Law:**

  A distinct change in the voluntary nature of ethical standards, principles and strategy maps, to the mandatory legislative action across different jurisdictions has been evident as part of the regulatory journey of many regions. Although the application of soft law remains a relevant practice in informing the rapidly evolving technology trends, a developing trend is that such standards are being supplemented or even replaced by statutes in the most risky AI applications.

- **Public Sector Governance:**

  It is also quite common that countries are more interested in implementing policies that will make the ethical and responsible application of AI technologies in their state administration institutions. These types of policies include the creation of regulations to shape the implementation of AI, the establishment of committees to coordinate work between ministries, and the implementation of AI systems to facilitate the provision of public services.

- **Sector-Specific Regulation:**

  Despite the fact that the area of basic horizontal AI-related laws is developing (primarily in Europe), an apparent trend towards regulating AI-related risks through sectoral legislation that is already in place or through new legislation tailored to this specific task in areas like finance, health care, transport and consumer protection can also be observed.

- **Response to Generative AI and Deepfakes:**

  The rapid development of AI technology and deepfake technology is appearing, and it also needs a regulation intervention that is rapid and specific in various locations. These regulatory measures involve labeling regulations of AI technology, countering fake information and addressing the problem of intellectual property and liability in the field of synthetic media. It demonstrates the rate and specificity of AI regulation development to keep up with the current technologies.

Regional Comparison

Although sharing similar tendencies, the global Al regulatory environment is also defined by the various regional approaches due to different socio-economic, legal, and geopolitical priorities.

- **Europe:** With its holistic, human-centric, and rights-focused framework for regulating AI, Europe is one of the world's top-ranking regions when it comes to AI governance. The AI Act, a landmark horizontal regulation from the EU, implements a rigorous risk-based regulatory approach that entails significant obligations for the use of potentially dangerous AI technologies and an absolute ban on using such technologies for their unethical purposes. A high maturity level is evident with a clear path towards enforcement. There is a heavy focus on rights, data protection (with GDPR playing an important role), and digital sovereignty, with the region taking up the mantle of the world's benchmark regulator. Non-EU countries tend to follow suit.

- **North America:** In the case of North America, especially with regard to its two primary actors, the USA and Canada, a vibrant and practical picture can be seen. It is not that much about creating an all-encompassing horizontal statute for the private sector (as seen in the EU) but rather a combination of various elements. First, it involves executive acts, use of current powers and laws, sectoral legislation, as well as the extensive use of 'soft law' tools, such as industry and voluntary standards. Moreover, both countries put forward a goal of promoting innovation and becoming global leaders in AI, alongside creating binding rules for governments' use of AI technology.

- **Central and South America:** In this part of the world, there is evidence of rapid maturation moving from initial ethical frameworks to developing binding frameworks. A human-centered perspective becomes crucial, with fundamental rights, democracy, and social equality taking precedence, and often draws heavily from the GDPR and the EU's AI Act. Brazil and Mexico stand out as two of the countries at the forefront of crafting governance frameworks. Topics include risk-based categorization, a focus on data protection, governance in the public sector when using AI, and increasingly digital sovereignty.

- **Asia:** The regulation of AI in Asia is extensive and very heterogeneous, ranging from technology giants to fast-growing economies. In general, the prevailing spirit is that of exploiting AI as an indispensable engine of economic growth, competitiveness, and digitization. While it might be possible that in some countries, there exists a complicated legal framework that embodies humanistic principles yet remains in the stage of soft law, even drawing upon the best international practices at times. A hybrid approach involving a combination of both general and specific laws related to digital matters. There is special attention paid to matters of national security and digital sovereignty (for those countries with state-led digital policies), as well as state involvement in building AI ecosystems. Generative AI reactions are rapid.

- **Middle East and North Africa (MENA):** MENA is fast developing as an AI region with a highly top-down government-led strategy that has become integral to the region's bold aspirations towards economic diversification and digitalization. Maturity in regulation has developed quickly, with the UAE and Saudi Arabia taking a lead with well-developed policies and the creation of AI agencies. Progress from soft law (principles and strategies) to binding legal instruments has been noted. Unifying trends in the region include national AI strategies, centralized governance, risk-based and human-centric approaches (inspired by the EU), innovative approaches to promoting technology (regulatory sandboxing), and a quest for digital and AI sovereignty (through indigenously developed AI).

- **Sub-Saharan Africa:** Sub-Saharan Africa is a rising frontier, marked by a notable move away from aspiration-driven digital economy frameworks towards a more focused risk-oriented approach to regulation. This is predominantly people-oriented and developmental in its orientation, with AI being viewed as a solution to prevailing social and economic problems in the region. There is a growing regulatory maturity here, with the presence of data protection legislation being the dominant horizontal legislation. National AI strategies are being formulated by nations that prioritize ethics, innovation, and digital sovereignty in order to foster an indigenous AI environment.

- **International Organizations:** Such organizations make up an important and well-established area in global AI governance, functioning as norm setters, facilitators, and harmonizers. These entities consider some basic elements such as the respect for human rights, democracy, and the rule of law. These entities are interested in conducting a dialogue between all parties and promoting international cooperation and interoperability. The activities carried out by these institutions involve international legal instruments (for instance, instruments approved by the Council of Europe) and international rules and guidelines that lack any binding effect (so-called soft law) (for example, OECD Principles on AI and UNESCO Recommendations on AI).

Convergence and Divergence

The international system of AI regulation exhibits multiple paths of development, which reach their highest point of connection through fundamental differences in regulatory methods and research priorities.

Convergence

- **Risk-Based Approaches:** This can be considered the most prominent commonality noted in the case. It appears that most regions are adopting a risk-based framework, which segments the use of AI based on the degree of risk. Such risks are often classified as unacceptable, high, medium, or low, accompanied by respective duties. In this regard, the AI Act from the EU has become extremely popular amongst other regions.

- **Human-Centric and Ethical Principles:** It is a consensus among all nations that ethicality should be at the core of artificial intelligence development and implementation. All the national policies, declarations, and laws from the researched areas put stress on values such as transparency, accountability, fairness, non-discrimination, respect for privacy, and human involvement in AI. The main objective here is to ensure that artificial intelligence respects human dignity and rights.
- **Data Protection as a Foundational Layer:** All the comprehensive data protection laws that exist or have been introduced not long ago, mostly based on the GDPR model, form a basis for AI regulation around the world. They control all important components associated with personal data management, including its collection, processing, and automated decision-making.
- **Promotion of Innovation:** While regulations may sometimes hamper innovation, it must be noted that globally, there is an understanding that innovation needs to be promoted in AI in order to keep up with other countries on the technology front. This can be accomplished via government investments in R&D, infrastructure development, and regulatory sandboxes.
- **Addressing Generative AI and Deepfakes:** fast-paced generative AI and deepfake growth has necessitated swift and converging initiatives. Many governments have started developing strategies to tackle content labeling, misinformation, and intellectual property rights associated with artificial media.
- **Public Sector Governance:** One standard way that governments have begun to regulate AI in various parts of the world is by creating strong governance structures for the proper use of AI, usually binding, within their government institutions, which helps to foster trust and set an example.

The Focus on Transparency and Accountability: No matter what model of regulation is employed, there is a sharp move in the international world towards increasing transparency in Al decision-making and accountable mechanisms, especially when it comes to the systems with effects on the rights or interests of individuals.

Divergence

- **Regulatory Approach (Horizontal vs. Hybrid/Sectoral):** Europe is unique in that it has adopted a horizontally oriented, holistic approach through the AI Act to create a single legal and binding framework for AI systems.
- This approach is different from that taken by North America, Asia, MENA, and Sub-Saharan Africa, which rely on hybrid or sector-specific approaches. Here, there is a combination of executive orders, soft laws, regulations in particular industries (such as finance and healthcare), and specific AI-focused laws without an overarching horizontal regulation.
- **Maturity and Pace of Implementation:** Europe exhibits strong regulatory development, with policies being translated into actions.
- North America is experiencing fast growth, with numerous policy initiatives.
- Central and South America, Asia (except some leaders), the Middle East and North Africa, and Sub-Saharan Africa are mainly at the emerging/transition stage, progressing from strategies and soft laws to hard laws, which are coupled with legislative measures.
- **Innovation vs. Precautionary Principle:** While all regions seek balance, there are nuanced differences in emphasis.
- Europe is inclined to take a position based on the precautionary approach, giving prominence to basic rights and security and

having an overarching regime that could be regarded as a more stringent one in some cases.

- North America and much of Asia, including MENA regions, tend to explicitly emphasize promoting innovation in AI and sustaining their global leadership role, initially preferring less regulatory approaches to prevent curbing technological progress.
- **Binding vs. Voluntary Measures for the Private Sector:** The EU's AI Act, for example, makes legally binding obligations on those who create and use AI technology, including the private sector, with strict sanctions if not complied with.
- North American countries tend to depend more on voluntary codes of conduct and industry best practices in the private sector, although some legislation may be introduced in certain areas.
- Currently, developing countries are in a phase of transition, going from soft to hard laws, albeit at different points.
- **Digital/AI Sovereignty:** The degree and form of digital/AI sovereignty exist as widely different trends worldwide.
    - Asian countries, MENA countries, and EU members operate an explicit policy framework that requires them to invest their national resources into developing domestic artificial intelligence systems and establishing data storage centers and national cloud computing facilities.
    - The United States national security interests take precedence in North America, yet different frameworks describe the "digital sovereignty" concept, which relates to national tech stacks.
- **State-Led vs. Market-Driven Approaches**:
    - **MENA** and most of Asia use a top-down approach driven by the state.

- North America, even with government participation, favors a market-led approach to innovation with government acting as a guide.

Key Challenges

The worldwide initiative to establish AI governance faces major difficulties because of the technology's complex nature, its fast-changing characteristics, and its deep impact on society.

- **Pace of Technological Advancement:** Another important issue that must be considered by legislation is that of the pace of technological advancement in the realm of artificial intelligence. It should be acknowledged that legislation moves much more slowly than any form of technology. As new technologies emerge, particularly the development of generative Al technologies, legislators feel as if they fall behind in the regulations.
- **Regulatory Fragmentation**: Though the emergence of distinct ways to regulate artificial intelligence in various states may be explained by individual preferences, it nevertheless poses considerable threats in terms of fragmentation. Businesses operate under pressure, innovations become restrained, international exchange of data is hampered, and the formation of global interoperability of artificial intelligence standards becomes less feasible due to the diverse ways in which this technology is regulated.
- **Enforcement and Implementation Capacity:** Nevertheless, the issue is not only the creation of the rule but the implementation of the law. In the case of artificial intelligence, the complexity of technology makes enforcing laws, conducting audits, and complying with regulations difficult. Why? Because those nations do not possess sufficient expertise, manpower, and resources.

- **Defining AI and its Scope:** One of the biggest challenges faced by AI has been a lack of adequate definition that clearly outlines what AI encompasses and helps draw the line between harmless applications and dangerous ones. As AI itself is very broad and rapidly evolving, there has been a case where harmless applications of AI are being controlled in a restrictive manner, while dangerous ones remain uncontrolled.

- **Cross-border Nature of AI:** The nature of AI technology and its underlying systems means that this technology is international. Models that were developed in one country can be operated all around the world. In addition, the data used to train AI models often belongs to numerous countries, making the international dimension very real and complicating the task of regulating AI on the national level.

- **Balancing Innovation and Risk Mitigation:** An equilibrium needs to be struck between the two – encouraging innovation, on one hand, and ensuring proper risk management, on the other. If regulation is too strict, especially if introduced at an early stage, this may stifle innovation. Too permissive measures may create risk, leading to losses, mistrust, and ultimately market failure.

- **Addressing Specific Harms (Bias, Discrimination, Privacy, Security):** The presence of existing biases in society may increase as a result of AI, and discrimination against certain individuals can ensue; secondly, the use of AI can cause a breach of privacy because it would gather data from diverse sources and analyze it based on different purposes; thirdly, new forms of cyber insecurity can arise. Handling such particular and sensitive harms requires sophisticated means.

- **Liability and Accountability:** It is hard to determine who bears responsibility when damage is caused by AI. Is it the creator, implementor, the source of data, or the end user? Current legal systems, such as product liability, might not suffice in determining accountability in autonomous and semi-autonomous Al systems.

- **Governance of Foundation Models and Generative Al:** The advent of foundation models and generative AI raises new issues in terms of governance. In light of their multipurpose applications, emergent features, and misuse potential, including spreading disinformation and creating deepfakes, different regulations will be needed to deal with such developments.
- **Bridging the Digital Divide and Ensuring Equitable Access:** Ensuring that artificial intelligence governance doesn't widen existing digital divides and that benefits from artificial intelligence are equally shared remains one of the biggest challenges faced by countries around the world. Technological colonization and widening global disparities have become serious issues that many developing countries cannot address without appropriate infrastructure and skills.

4.2 Data Governance and Legal Compliance

In the current digital era, data is the greatest asset for all types of organizations, irrespective of their sectors. To make effective decision-making, operate effectively, and deliver personalized service, organizations require data to a large extent. There are major challenges related to the governance of data, its security, and compliance with laws. At this stage, the governance of data and compliance with laws becomes of paramount importance.

The concept of "data governance" refers to the framework that establishes principles, processes, policies, and controls required to ensure that the data is accurate, trustworthy, secure, and utilized correctly. On the other hand, legal compliance pertains to the adherence to all relevant regulations, rules, and standards in collecting, processing, storing, and transferring data. By combining these two concepts, organizations can accomplish their strategic objectives, manage risks, and maintain their trustworthiness among their clients by managing data effectively.

Why data governance matters

Data is abundant within modern enterprises. However, without a systematic method of handling this large quantity of data, it soon begins to become disorganized, imprecise, and susceptible to compromise. This could render the once useful data obsolete under the stringent laws of privacy protection.

This is achieved through data governance, which sets out protocols for ensuring data consistency, safety, and integrity. It is through this that the costs of rectifying errors, regulatory issues, and other such problems can be minimized, thus creating room for enhanced analysis and decision-making.

Key components of data governance

There are a handful of essential components to good data governance that guarantee the integrity and safety of data. All the way from its inception to its eventual deletion, these essential parts of data governance cooperate to control data. Learn how these fundamental data governance pillars support data consistency, mitigate risks, and uncover vital business insights.

- **Data rules and regulations**

  The rules and laws of data governance outline the processes by which an organization gathers, stores, retrieves, and shares data. Precise controls guarantee that all data conforms with applicable rules, supporting privacy and security standards. Good data governance rules also should not remain static. Regular updates are key to adapting to new operational and compliance requirements.

- **Data quality**

  The usability, timeliness, accuracy, completeness, and consistency of data are all indicators of its quality. These high standards can only be maintained through regulations and systems, which fall under data governance. Data cleaning, validation, monitoring, and standardization are some of the techniques and tools involved. The occurrence of data errors, redundancies, and inconsistencies can be minimized with structured data quality management.

- **Data stewardship**

  Data stewardship can be defined as the individual role that is involved with maintaining the quality, integrity, and usability of information within the enterprise. Data stewards serve as custodians of selected data areas to ensure compliance and proper utilization of information by different groups and to oversee the quality of the data used.

- **Data compliance**

  Data compliance guarantees that data is managed according to the rules and regulations that apply in the particular industry or field. It means observing the laws relating to privacy, security, and auditing of the data. Data auditing plays a crucial role in ensuring compliance. Through auditing, problems can be identified in terms of how data is handled or accessed.

- **Data cataloging**

  In order to get insightful knowledge about any business, the first step is locating relevant data sources. This is achieved through cataloging, which involves listing all data-related materials that may be found within a company in a systematic way so that users can easily locate and curate the data they require.

- **Data monitoring**

  Data monitoring refers to the tracking and evaluation of data-related activities against established quality and security standards. The process requires two steps which include validating new data and detecting anomalies and controlling user permissions. The organization continuously monitors its operations to decrease compliance risks and maintain data integrity which enables better decision-making.

How data governance works

Data governance includes a series of processes that ensure the consistency and security of data. Each process, from role allocation to the integration of technology, contributes to laying the groundwork for accountability and flexibility. Here are the essential processes you must undertake to establish effective data governance programs.

1. **Establish a data governance framework**

   Develop a strategic blueprint that defines the operational procedures for data governance throughout the organization. The existence of an effective data governance framework enables teams to work together toward a common objective. A practical data governance framework should include:

   - **Objective and scope**: Define which data domains will be governed and why.
   - **Organizational structure:** Outline a clear data governance operating model that determines how data decisions will flow through the organization.
   - **Data standards:** Document clear standards and metrics for managing data.
   - **Processes and workflows:** Identify key operational steps for handling data throughout its lifecycle.
   - **Data technology**: Specify tools needed to automate and support key governance tasks.

2. **Outline clear data governance policies**

   With a clear data governance framework in place, introduce policies that translate these high-level standards into actionable rules for day-to-day tasks. This includes detailed orders for managing data quality, compliance, privacy, and security. Clear policies reduce operational ambiguity, allowing teams to comply confidently with regulatory requirements.

3. **Assign data governance roles and responsibilities**

   Clear responsibilities and avoidance of ambiguity can be achieved by outlining distinct data governance roles. On a daily basis, certain data assets are overseen by data stewards. Along with these important data governance responsibilities are:

   - **Data governance committee:** Provides strategic oversight, approves data governance policies, and resolves conflicts across data domains.
   - **Data owners:** Oversee the accuracy, quality, and consistency of specific datasets, and authorize data access and use.
   - **Data custodians:** Implement technical data security controls, including data encryption, data access controls, and data privacy.
   - **Data users:** Consume data responsibly according to governance policies and report any discrepancies or issues.

4. **Implement data governance processes**

   Data creation, management, and protection over its lifecycle can be better accomplished with well-defined procedures. For the sake of trust, risk mitigation, and regulatory compliance, standardized processes are essential. Important steps in data governance comprise:

- **Data classification:** Categorize data based on sensitivity, usage, and regulatory requirements to determine appropriate handling and protection measures.
- **Access control:** Define and enforce who can view, edit, or share specific datasets to maintain security and prevent unauthorized use.
- **Data governance documentation:** Record processes to create transparency and enable operational consistency across teams.
- **Data validation**: The process uses tools to check whether data meets established quality standards and format requirements before storage and usage, which leads to better accuracy and dependable results.
- **Incident resolution:** The organization needs to develop procedures that will enable staff members to identify data errors or breaches and report them while maintaining an effective system for handling such incidents.

5. **Adopt data governance technologies**

   The adoption of appropriate data platforms is key to scaling data governance policies and procedures. Today's advanced data platforms can help streamline operations and compliance, and gain visibility about your organization's data. With the support of such technologies, you will be able to lessen the workload and boost your precision.

6. **Conduct audits and foster continuous improvements**

   Data governance needs periodic assessment and improvement. Regularly conduct audits and improve policies and processes. The quality control process must confirm the validity, integrity, and consistency of your data sets. Also, stakeholder feedback will be useful for adapting to changing business goals.

Importance of Data Governance

Data governance does not just serve as a technical activity but is also an essential strategy that needs to be adopted. The significance of data governance can be explained with the help of the following factors:

- **Improved Decision-Making**: With quality data, one can make sound and well-informed decisions.
- **Regulatory Compliance**: Through governance structures, organizations are able to adhere to legal compliance.
- **Risk Management**: Good governance practices mitigate any risk posed by breaches or misuse of data.
- **Operational Efficiency**: Standardization of processes enhances efficiency through reduced redundancy.
- **Trust and Transparency**: Customers and stakeholders are more likely to trust organizations that handle data responsibly.

Legal Compliance in Data Management

Data handling must be done in accordance with all applicable rules and regulations in order to be considered legally compliant. The purpose of these rules is to prevent unauthorized access to personal information and to make sure that businesses act properly when dealing with customer data.

Key Data Protection Regulations

1. **General Data Protection Regulation (GDPR):** Any business dealing with the private information of EU residents must comply with the General Data Protection Regulation (GDPR). It stresses the importance of people's rights over their data, openness, and permission.

2. **California Consumer Privacy Act (CCPA):** The CCPA gives Californians some rights with respect to their personal data, such as the ability to access, erase, and refuse data sale.

3. **Health Insurance Portability and Accountability Act (HIPAA):** The Health Insurance Portability and Accountability Act (HIPAA) control the storage and transmission of protected health information inside the United States.

4. **Information Technology Act, 2000 (India):** In India, the IT Act provides legal recognition for electronic transactions and includes provisions for data protection and cybersecurity.

5. **Digital Personal Data Protection Act (India):** This recent legislation focuses on protecting personal data and outlines obligations for data fiduciaries and rights for individuals.

Key Principles of Legal Compliance

Legal compliance in data governance is guided by several fundamental principles:

1. **Lawfulness, Fairness, and Transparency:** The data shall be collected and processed in an ethical manner.

2. **Purpose Limitation:** The data is supposed to be used for the purpose intended.

3. **Data Minimization:** Organizational entities shall only collect information that is needed for business activities.

4. **Accuracy:** The data shall be accurate.

5. **Storage Limitation:** No information should be stored beyond what is required.

6. **Integrity and Confidentiality:** The data should be well secured from any sort of breach.

Relationship Between Data Governance and Legal Compliance

There is an interrelationship between data governance and legal compliance. Legal compliance ensures that these processes are in accordance with the law, whereas data governance forms the basis of data management.

- **Governance Enables Compliance**: A robust governance framework ensures that data practices adhere to regulations.
- **Compliance Drives Governance**: Legal requirements often shape governance policies and procedures.
- **Shared Objectives**: Both aim to protect data, ensure accountability, and maintain trust.

For example, a governance policy requiring encryption of sensitive data supports compliance with data protection laws that mandate security measures.

Challenges in Data Governance and Compliance

Organizations face several challenges in implementing effective data governance and ensuring compliance:

1. **Data Silos:** Data is often stored in separate systems, making it difficult to manage and govern effectively.
2. **Rapid Data Growth:** The exponential increase in data volume makes it challenging to maintain quality and security.
3. **Complex Regulatory Landscape:** Different countries have varying data protection laws, making compliance complicated for global organizations.
4. **Lack of Awareness and Training:** Employees may not fully understand data governance policies or legal requirements.

5. **Technological Complexity:** Implementing governance tools and systems requires significant investment and expertise.
6. **Cybersecurity Threats:** Increasing cyberattacks pose risks to data security and compliance.

Best Practices for Effective Data Governance

To overcome these challenges, organizations should adopt the following best practices:

1. **Establish a Data Governance Framework:** Define clear policies, roles, and responsibilities for data management.
2. **Implement Strong Data Security Measures:** Use encryption, access controls, and monitoring systems to protect data.
3. **Ensure Data Quality:** Regularly audit and clean data to maintain accuracy and consistency.
4. **Promote a Data-Driven Culture:** Encourage employees to understand and follow data governance practices.
5. **Leverage Technology:** Use data governance tools and platforms to automate processes and improve efficiency.
6. **Conduct Regular Compliance Audits:** Assess adherence to legal requirements and identify areas for improvement.

Role of Technology in Data Governance and Compliance

Technology plays a crucial role in enabling effective data governance and compliance:

- **Data Management Platforms**: These tools help manage data across its lifecycle.

- **Artificial Intelligence (AI)**: AI can automate data classification, monitoring, and anomaly detection.
- **Blockchain**: Provides secure and transparent data transactions.
- **Cloud Computing**: Offers scalable solutions for data storage and management.

However, the use of advanced technologies also requires careful consideration of privacy and security implications.

Ethical Considerations in Data Governance

Beyond legal compliance, organizations must consider ethical aspects of data usage. Ethical data governance involves:

- Respecting individuals' privacy
- Avoiding bias in data analysis and decision-making
- Ensuring transparency in data practices
- Using data for socially responsible purposes

Ethical considerations are particularly important in areas such as artificial intelligence, where biased data can lead to unfair outcomes.

Future Trends in Data Governance and Compliance

The landscape of data governance and legal compliance is continuously evolving. Key trends include:

1. **Stronger Regulations:** Governments are introducing stricter data protection laws worldwide.
2. **Increased Focus on Privacy:** Consumers are becoming more aware of their data rights and demanding greater transparency.

3. **Integration of AI in Governance:** AI will play a larger role in automating governance processes.
4. **Cross-Border Data Regulations:** Managing data across jurisdictions will become increasingly complex.
5. **Zero-Trust Security Models:** Organizations are adopting zero-trust approaches to enhance data security.

4.3 Sector-Specific AI Regulatory Requirements

The emergence of AI technology has brought changes in the functioning and decision-making process of organizations, along with the manner in which their operations benefit their customers. Be it the healthcare sector, banking sector, transportation, etc., AI technology is finding application in several domains and has become indispensable. Issues such as privacy, biases, accountability, safety, and the ethical use of technology are some of the many issues faced by such technologies. Since every sector faces a unique set of challenges and threats, there cannot be a single rule that can help regulate all these sectors. It is for this reason that we have sector-specific AI regulation rules.

Industry-specific AI regulations should aim at encouraging responsible use of AI systems while ensuring that innovation and competitiveness are not compromised. Such regulatory measures may include guidelines developed on the basis of general regulations for data protection and AI management, but with more detailed stipulations depending on the particular industry involved. The AI technology requires compliance with strict requirements for safety and accuracy when used in the health sector, but needs to protect customer data before all other obligations in marketing.

The healthcare sector has stringent regulations regarding the use of AI technology that relates to numerous other sectors. The AI applications in healthcare are used in medical imaging, diagnostics, drug discovery, and patient monitoring. It is because all these areas have direct implications on people that safety, reliability and precision become the primary consideration when it comes to regulation. An AI solution must undergo testing processes since it will be certified after successful functioning is proven. AI systems that act as medical devices have to go through numerous certification procedures in terms of their classification. Another area where there should be strict adherence to a particular rule is the protection of health data and the appropriate handling of personal data. Physicians and nurses need to have transparency regarding AI systems since they must be aware of the rationale behind certain suggestions of the given systems. The ethical concerns that prevail in health care facilities pose further challenges in the attempt to develop AI regulations.

The financial services sector also has a high level of importance of AI legislation. Banking, insurance and investment agencies use artificial intelligence to support their customers, conclude transactions using algorithms, detect fraud cases, and analyze loans. This sector is regulated on accountability, transparency and justice. There should be no discrimination on the basis of gender, skin color or social background of the people, as it would cause unfair evaluation of the loans in the lending industry. Also, financial institutions must clarify to their customers the rationale of algorithms. The information that has a high value is always personal financial data, hence the consideration of data protection in this instance. The legislation of artificial intelligence (AI) in this area is difficult due to the anti-money laundering (AML) requirements.

The retail and e-commerce sector is one of the fields that heavily relies on artificial intelligence technology to provide individualized services, including recommendations, advertisements, demand forecasts, and price adjustments. Although these applications may offer various applications that are beneficial, they make people nervous about their private data being misused. Regulatory frameworks within this sector of business underline the need to have the consent of consumers before they can use their personal information. Companies ought to clarify to consumers how the AI systems process the activity of the consumer and suggest recommendations. Algorithm pricing is another aspect of discussion as far as artificial intelligence is used in this sphere of business. That is, AI systems could be in a position to manipulate prices based on the profile of the customer. Regulators have become more and more interested in this practice due to its potential to exploit consumers. Businesses must also ensure that AI systems will not promote any discrimination or will not give biased results.

The retail and e-commerce sector is one of the fields that heavily relies on artificial intelligence technology to provide individualized services, including recommendations, advertisements, demand forecasts, and price adjustments. Although these applications may offer various applications that are beneficial, they make people nervous about their private data being misused. Regulatory frameworks within this sector of business underline the need to have the consent of consumers before they can use their personal information. Companies ought to clarify to consumers how the AI systems process the activity of the consumer and suggest recommendations. Algorithm pricing is another aspect of discussion as far as artificial intelligence is used in this sphere of business. That is, AI systems could be in a position to manipulate prices based on the profile of the customer. Regulators have become more and more interested in this practice due to its potential to exploit consumers. Businesses must also ensure that AI systems will not promote any discrimination or will not give biased results.

The government has found a lot of use for artificial intelligence in areas like administration, social services, prevention of crimes, and governance, among others. Although AI could enhance efficiency and make more effective decisions, its application poses a number of problems in terms of transparency, accountability, and privacy. The regulations in this sector are based on equity and non-discrimination, especially when it comes to predictive policing and the distribution of welfare. It is the government's responsibility to see to it that AI does not continue to propagate discrimination and injustice. The citizens have a right to know anything that concerns them; therefore, transparency is necessary. Sometimes, citizens should have the capacity to challenge or reverse the decisions made by systems operated by AI. It is important to protect the integrity of data and safeguard the privacy of citizens' personal data.

Another area where AI is taking its toll is the education sector. The technology is used to learn in a customized way, mark out tests, evaluate student performance, and manage work with the help of AI. Ensuring the impartiality of exams conducted through AI and the security of data belonging to the students are the main regulatory issues in this area. Academic institutions should not lead to bias in the deployment of AI in grading and evaluation purposes. Teachers and students must understand the impact that AI can have on the end-of-course results of their courses; therefore, transparency is essential. Issues of data manipulation and monitoring of students require the utmost consideration. Regulatory bodies are increasingly stressing the need to deploy AI in educational activities in a responsible manner to provide equal opportunities to all learners.

Applications for artificial intelligence (AI) exist in many different industries including robotics, quality management, logistics planning, predictive maintenance, among others. Rules and regulations regarding the use of AI in industry and manufacturing revolve around safety, reliability, and security. The AI system should adhere to industrial safety regulations to avoid any hazards that could affect the well-being of employees. It is common for the industrial system to become a target of cyber threats, thus emphasizing the importance of having security measures in place. Security measures would not only ensure protection but operational stability as well. It is also important to consider the social and economic consequences of automation due to possible job losses through AI technology.

Despite the divergent nature of the different industries, there are some regulations that apply to artificial intelligence regardless of where it is used. Regulation issues related to security, risk management, discrimination, transparency, accountability and governance, and privacy are among those that are covered here. Businesses should ensure that their artificial intelligence systems meet these requirements. This will form the basis for an ethical use of artificial intelligence technology.

Key Sector-Specific Regulatory Requirements

The regulations for Artificial Intelligence (AI) usage in India have come from each respective sector to strike a balance between safety and innovation. Regulatory guidelines for AI have been put out in various sectors, such as the digital platforms sector, health care, insurance, the educational sector, and the financial services sector. The primary aim of the regulations is to achieve ethical, secure and responsible AI use and reduce risks that are specific to specific industries.

The Reserve Bank of India (RBI) regulates and supervises the financial services sector and this includes fintech and banking. The RBI has implemented extremely stringent rules in the cybersecurity, data protection, and operational resiliency domains, especially with respect to financial services that rely heavily on artificial intelligence technologies. Cyber resilience frameworks guarantee that any organization within the financial services domain that makes use of AI technology in its automated decision-making, fraud-detection, and credit-scoring processes is protected against any kind of breach or loss of sensitive information. Furthermore, the AI system used must guarantee that the lending process is fair and unbiased. Moreover, customers are entitled to an explanation of any automated output, and the bank must disclose its algorithmic approach to decision-making.

This industry is regulated by the Insurance Regulatory and Development Authority of India (IRDAI), which provides thorough guidelines for information security and cybersecurity. As artificial intelligence gets used in processes such as underwriting, risk assessment, and claims processing, it is essential that the insurers maintain high levels of accuracy and consistency in the collection of data. As per IRDAI guidelines, it is necessary to maintain high standards of data protection during the process of using AI systems. The key aspect to consider here is the development of unbiased and fair AI models for underwriting purposes. The same holds true for the process of claims processing since it involves the use of AI to ensure there are no wrongful rejections of claims.

Patient safety, confidentiality of data, and correctness of the procedure are matters of primary concern for the healthcare and HealthTech industry. Validation of diagnostic tools, artificial intelligence in radiology, and predictive health care procedures is essential to ensure the accuracy of the process. Sometimes, regulatory measures include compliance with current health-related laws, especially the PC-PNDT Act. It is important that AI systems maintain high standards of accuracy to prevent misdiagnosis. Another issue of concern within the realm of healthcare services is the protection of personal data from any leakage by healthcare providers and the use of such data strictly within its intended scope of application. Actually, medical expert-witness advice may also be beneficial, given that AI systems provide interpreted information.

The education sector uses artificial intelligence to create personalized learning experiences, assess student performance and to manage administrative work. The use of artificial intelligence technologies needs human supervision according to established regulatory requirements. AI technology should assist teachers in developing their professional skills instead of taking over their teaching responsibilities. We strongly advise educational institutions to protect themselves from any chances of AI algorithms curbing students' creativity and biasing their assessments. Educational institutions handle sensitive student information, which creates a requirement for data privacy protection. The law requires educational institutions to treat student data with responsible and ethical handling.

AI is extensively used by digital platforms for such purposes as content moderation, recommendations, and user engagement. AI systems used by platforms for such purposes are covered by the Intermediary Guidelines and Information Technology Act 2000. It is important for platforms to make sure that their AI tools do not support any content that might be regarded as unlawful or unethical. Platforms are supposed to develop such tools that will help them monitor content, offer redressals for grievances, and safeguard users' interests. Moderation systems based on AI should be transparent and accountable. In particular, there should be ways for users to appeal decisions related to content removal or account blocking.

Key regulatory requirements across these sectors can be summarized as follows:

- Strong **cybersecurity and data protection frameworks** to safeguard sensitive information
- Ensuring **fairness and non-discrimination** in AI-driven decision-making
- Maintaining **transparency and explainability** of AI systems
- Implementing **accountability and audit mechanisms** for AI processes
- Ensuring **human oversight** in critical applications
- Compliance with **sector-specific laws and regulatory guidelines**
- Protecting **consumer and user rights**, including grievance redressal mechanisms
- Promoting **ethical and responsible use of AI technologies**

4.4 Cross-Border Data and AI Governance Challenges

As regards contemporary economies that are tightly interconnected, information is free to flow from one jurisdiction to another, thus enabling global business operations, cloud technologies, and innovative applications of Artificial Intelligence (AI). An increasing number of organizations take advantage of information flows between countries when training AI algorithms, delivering services, and cooperating globally. While it is easy for information to be transmitted cross-border, it faces serious barriers in the sphere of data governance since countries have distinct requirements regarding data gathering, processing, storing, and transmission.

Data transfer across borders is important since it allows for innovations that will be very useful for AI technologies, because large amounts of data are needed for the successful processing and delivery of results. International firms use cloud computing across the world for processing their data due to scalability and Big Data analysis capabilities. But at the same time, these procedures may pose risks in relation to data transfers across different jurisdictions. Governments are increasingly concerned about data sovereignty, national security, and the protection of citizens' personal information, leading to stricter controls on international data transfers.

Deregulation of regulations is a major obstacle to effective cross-border data governance. Examples of various laws related to data protection can be seen around the globe; the GDPR in Europe, sector-specific legislation in America, and ever-evolving data protection legislation in India are only some of them. Each of these legislations differs in terms of data localization requirements, user rights, enforcement mechanisms, and the required consent. The end result is that multinational corporations find themselves navigating through a complex maze of laws and regulations, making compliance extremely difficult and forcing them to implement a myriad of compliance measures simultaneously. This fragmented approach in AI deployment has resulted in confusion and increased costs.

Data localization policies represent yet another difficult barrier; in some nations, the government itself mandates the storing and processing of particular types of data inside its own territories. While the intention behind this is noble, these rules can also serve to interfere with the working of AI globally, as well as with international collaboration efforts. For instance, AI programs that are trained on local datasets tend to be less diverse in nature, thus reducing their efficacy and generalizability. Moreover, data localization could turn out to be expensive because data centers have to be set up in multiple nations.

It is equally important that the functions of privacy and data protection be considered in cross-border data governance. It is possible that different levels of protection may apply to data being transferred across borders, and this might affect people's right to privacy. Especially when dealing with sensitive data such as bank information or medical records, the huge challenge of protecting data and preventing its misuse without authorization comes into the picture.

The ethical and governance challenges posed by artificial intelligence will become even more complex in the future. If machine learning algorithms use information from multiple countries, they can have cultural prejudices or imbalances that might be unethical in certain contexts. For instance, an algorithm created in one part of the world may not conform to the laws and ethics in another area. Additionally, the question of ensuring that AI systems are made transparent and explainable in operations not limited by borders also exists.

Cybersecurity threats create significant challenges for international data transmission. The process of transferring data between networks and international borders becomes vulnerable to multiple cyber threats, which include security breaches and hacking attempts. Organizations need to establish comprehensive cybersecurity systems, which include their data transfer procedures, their monitoring systems and their emergency response strategies. The problem exists because different countries maintain distinct cybersecurity rules, which create security risks for organizations.

However, another challenge lies in the field of legal jurisdiction. When it comes to data breaches or violations of regulations, one would encounter complications in deciding the appropriate legal framework that would oversee such an offense. Conflicts in jurisdiction will arise since multiple states would want to govern particular sets of information. These conflicts will hamper enforcement efforts and cause problems for the company. Punitive differences will further add to the difficulties.

Moreover, without the presence of global standards and harmonization, the challenge will be further complicated. Despite the efforts of international institutions to come up with uniform standards, there are still notable differences among them. The lack of guidelines will make compliance impossible for the company. Efforts towards harmonization are being made, but at a very slow pace.

Concepts to Know About Cross-Border AI Governance

Before we dive into detailing the cross-border AI regulations in place, it's important to understand the following concepts:

- **Cross-Border AI Systems**: Artificial intelligence that operates across more than one legal boundary
- **Data Localization**: Legal or regulatory restrictions that mandate that specific data (e.g. financial, personal, or government data) be stored and processed within a country's borders
- **Jurisdictional Conflicts:** Conditions where complying with one set of regulations or laws simultaneously prevents meeting another set of regulations or laws

Regulatory Arbitrage: The Regulatory Reality Check

- **United States:** A Complex Mixture of AI Regulation

  The United States lacks a standardized legal framework for the regulation of artificial intelligence (AI), analogous to state taxation but pertaining to AI's underlying code and behaviors. However, 22 out of 260 AI-related bills had their way into the US Senate in 2025. Neither will the increasing number of laws and regulations pertaining to artificial intelligence. The number of artificial intelligence (AI)-related legislative proposals examined by states increased from 700 in 2024 to an even higher total in 2025.

  Patchwork nightmares are born from this concoction of new regulations. When Colorado's comprehensive AI bill was vetoed, the state took a different approach, passing a series of targeted laws that dealt with issues like election deepfakes, warnings about AI-generated content, digital copies of performers, and disclosure of training data.

- **EU:** One Ring to Rule Them All

  However, the EU has approached matters from an entirely new perspective by passing the AI Act, the world's first legal framework for AI. Moreover, companies based in the United States should know that while the AI Act is applicable to organizations in the EU, it can also be applied to organizations outside the EU whose AI systems or results are used within the EU.

  However, the setting of restrictions on "unacceptable risk" artificial intelligence techniques for all 27 member states of the European Union beginning on February 2, 2025, and the subsequent implementation of additional restrictions until 2027 makes this Act's timeline rather aggressive.

- **China:** State-Controlled with Global Ambitions

  The traditional law of China stresses the significance of the state as well as culture, while also embracing province and city legislation. The technology that utilizes artificial intelligence, including content suggestion, speech recognition, and text recognition software, must obtain government approval before being made available in China. This is even more challenging on an international level.

When Laws Collide: Examples of Real-World Battle Royals

- **The OpenAI Data Dilemma:** David vs. Goliath vs. GDPR

  In May 2025, there was an issuance of a preservation order made by a federal court in the US to preserve all ChatGPT discussion logs on the part of OpenAI. The directive concerns more than 400 million users globally. Adhering to a preservation order coming from the US could be in direct contravention of Articles 5 and 17 of the GDPR, resulting in a serious conflict.

Consider this, for example: The right to be forgotten, formulated in Article 17 GDPR (originally in the Data Protection Directive of 1995), is quite out of place alongside the detailed discovery provisions in U.S. litigation. The use of artificial intelligence technology makes the situation even more difficult, owing to the amount of personal information processed by these systems.

This will have a great impact on the firm. Although there had been commitments of privacy protection made by organizations and their vendors for AI, the new data exposure laws may prove to be a difficult task for firms that use OpenAI and other such companies as their AI vendors.

- **TikTok:** The Multi-Jurisdictional Nightmare

  The same platform faced an ideal convergence of regulations by ByteDance: data localization policies owing to the national security interests of the United States, export licenses for AI technologies in China, and GDPR requirements in Europe.

- **Clearview AI:** When Enforcement Goes Global

  The DPA of the Netherlands imposed a fine. Despite the company's statement of not offering services in the EU, the court imposed a fine of €30.5 million on Clearview for violating GDPR. It proves how companies that believe themselves safe from a country's jurisdiction may still end up paying fines for violating their privacy laws.

- **The Business Impact:** More Than Compliance Theater

  Regulatory complexity has added another layer of difficulty to healthcare compliance, which was already challenging for enterprises. While AI is generally considered a SaMD (Software as a Medical Device) by most frameworks, the data acquired by devices and AI evolves over time, and the meaning of Personally Identifiable Information differs across jurisdictions.

A compliance matrix that would make any governance, security, or compliance expert nervous would result from adding HIPAA compliance standards to GDPR mandates and state-specific AI rules.

- **The Outsourcing Fallacy**

  You can't hire someone else to be legally responsible; that much is certain. It's as if you were a dry cleaner who sent their customers' shirts to a handyman for fixing. The client will still hold you responsible, not the contractor, in the event that the contractor damages the shirt or causes other issues. You can't escape responsibility for your actions in data management, and you're ultimately answerable to your consumers.

What C-Suite Leaders Can Do Today: Action Over Analysis Paralysis

1. **Immediate Risk Assessment (Over the Next 30 Days)**

   Inventory your AI exposure:

   - Map AI systems affecting international users
   - Identify AI systems that might touch the EU market and assess their risk level
   - Document data flows and retention policies
   - Understand which jurisdictions' laws apply to your systems

   Conduct red flag analysis to look for systems that:

   - Collect psychological or behavioral data, target specific demographic groups, make automated decisions affecting access to services, or process biometric information

- Process EU resident data (triggering EU AI Act requirements)
- Handle protected health information
- Make "consequential decisions" under various state laws

2. **Technical Architecture Solutions (Over the Next 90 Days)**

   Privacy-preserving technologies:

   - Implement federated learning to avoid cross-border data transfers
   - Deploy differential privacy techniques
   - Use privacy-focused modules to ensure compliance with diverse data protection laws

   Modular compliance architecture:

   - Create region-specific AI model versions
   - Build configurable governance frameworks
   - Design systems that can adapt to different jurisdictional requirements without complete rebuilds

3. **Legal and Organizational Strategies (Ongoing)**

   Representative Appointments:

   - Providers of high-risk AI systems established outside the EU must appoint an authorized representative in the EU in writing. Don't wait. This requirement is already in effect for many systems.
   - Legal caveat: This is for non-EU AI providers that place their high-risk AI systems or general-purpose AI models on the EU market.

Unified Governance Frameworks:

- Establish AI governance that addresses multiple jurisdictions simultaneously rather than creating separate compliance programs. Organizations can best benefit from a single, focused approach to safeguarding data and addressing AI-related cybersecurity threats.

Contract Redesign:

- Add vendor notification requirements for litigation holds.
- Include terms requiring notification when data becomes subject to a hold, including a court-mandated hold, and providing opportunities to object to disclosure.
- Build in jurisdiction-specific termination clauses.
- Plan for conflicting legal requirements scenarios.

4. **Strategic Policy Engagement (6-12 Months)**

Industry Collaboration:

- Support harmonization efforts and mutual recognition agreements. Like-minded governments should work together to implement basic data-transfer agreements that establish guidelines for how companies handle cross-border user-data transfers.

Standards Development:

- Engage with international standards bodies working on AI governance harmonization. Aligning technical standards can significantly reduce compliance complexity.

4.5 Preparing for Future Regulatory Developments

Regulators are trying hard to cope with the rapidly evolving domain of data technology and Artificial Intelligence (AI). All this is happening due to the intent to minimize any potential threats and ethical and societal consequences associated with them. The problem of establishing a strong regulatory mechanism that will make sure AI algorithms are reliable, transparent, and responsible has become ever more popular with government bodies, business organizations, and international bodies. However, this question creates both opportunities and challenges for businesses because building resilience, reliability, and sustainability in a constantly changing legal environment becomes more important than mere anticipation of changes.

These are some of the main factors that make it important for enterprises to gear themselves up for future regulations. There have been several nations across the world that are working towards creating and modifying the legislation pertaining to AI. Moreover, there are ongoing changes in the regulatory landscape, keeping pace with AI. In this context, it can be stated that the European Union AI Act is one of the best examples, where the AI systems have been categorized depending on the level of risk involved, and their impact and responsibilities have been defined accordingly.

The only strategy that can ensure readiness in relation to the future regulation is being proactive and taking the necessary actions in advance. In other words, an organization must consider the future trend of regulation and adjust its internal processes, as well as ensure that compliance has been integrated into the operation of the business itself. The process of compliance cannot be perceived as an isolated action, but rather, something that grows together with technology.

Thus, the creation of a comprehensive governance structure of AI is going to be the first move towards it. It is imperative that there are well-defined and agreed-upon responsibilities and obligations in terms of the use of AI within the organization. These will include regulations regarding the management of data, the assessment of risks and considerations about ethics.

The development of AI governance practices will enable the organization to be prepared for regulation in the present day and in the future.

Further, it is also important to ensure that incorporating ethics in the application of artificial intelligence is taken into consideration. In the future, more emphasis should be put on ensuring that the creation of AI involves certain aspects such as non-discrimination, accountability, transparency, and justice. It is important to ensure that when creating an AI system, corporations incorporate ethical considerations. This will allow for what is referred to as "ethics by design." By following this process, companies will be able to deal with regulatory changes effectively while minimizing compliance issues.

Another area of focus will be data governance and privacy management, since this allows for anticipation of regulatory requirements. As regulations concerning data protection become more stringent, it is important to ensure that companies adopt effective measures in terms of data governance. This includes reducing the use of data, secure storage of data, and limited access to data. When dealing with data, it is important to incorporate privacy by design and privacy by default.

Risk assessment and impact analysis represent another necessary requirement for businesses. Risk assessments carried out regularly will help identify different kinds of risks linked with AI technology. For example, there could be problems with biases and security. AI impact assessment and algorithmic audits are becoming increasingly popular within regulatory compliance. Not only do they help manage the risks, but they also prove that due diligence has been performed by the business, thus making them beneficial for regulatory compliance.

Another critical element of being ready for the future pertains to transparency and explainability. The necessity of transparent reasoning as to the workings of an AI will arise in mission-critical situations in the areas of healthcare, finance, and policing. Businesses will be mandated in the future to provide an explanation about why AI has reached certain decisions. Companies will need to invest in XAI approaches to make the decision-making process more transparent.

It is imperative to educate and train workers so as to be prepared to meet future regulatory changes. Organizations have the obligation to provide their workers with education concerning the legal, ethical, and practical aspects of AI governance. Issues such as information security, minimizing biases, and ethical usage of AI are just some of the important topics that should be covered in training. Both compliance and adequate response to regulation are better facilitated through educating people.

Networks and cooperation with external parties are yet another significant aspect that should be considered. To be aware of the recent innovations in the sphere under consideration, it is necessary to ensure that an organization has a network that maintains contacts with universities, industries, and the government. Through cooperation via forums and consultations, one may get valuable information on forthcoming legislation.

The importance of technology in ensuring that compliance is achieved cannot be overstated. Regarding the management, monitoring, and auditing of data, it will be important for the firm to take advantage of new technologies. By leveraging AI-powered systems in its governance processes, not only will the firm be able to increase efficiency but also be able to achieve compliance within the set timeframe.

Preparing for Regulatory Change

In the fast-paced, ever-evolving world of finance and technology, so are the regulatory regimes. Companies should always be prepared for regulatory changes to ensure compliance and competitiveness. This is no longer simply a response-driven process but a strategic one that requires foresight and flexibility. Here are some important strategies that firms can adopt to prepare for regulatory change.

1. **Prioritizing Continuous Education**

   There is an increasing dynamism in the regulatory environment as more and more rules and amendments are made with ever-increasing speed. It is widely recognized by industry specialists that the regulation level reaches its peak, the need for education becomes apparent.

   In order to stay within the boundaries of the existing legislation, a company has to participate in constant educational activities. The employees have to attend various courses, seminars and training programs to learn about the latest regulations and ways to comply with them.

   In addition to that, a learning culture in a company makes it possible to predict future changes in the regulatory framework.

2. **Building Robust Internal and External Networks**

   Collaboration internally with various teams and externally with other parties is important for dealing with the challenges associated with regulations. Collaboration internally within front, middle, and back offices is important for communication purposes.

   Collaboration externally with regulators, custodians, experts, and other parties will make access to the necessary data easier. Collaboration with regulators will help companies understand their expectations and deal with potential problems before they arise.

   For example, launching a new financial instrument or investment product may benefit from the involvement of a variety of teams, including portfolio managers, risk managers, and operations staff, thus ensuring smooth information exchange.

3. **Automating Regulatory Reporting**

Regulatory reporting is an enormous challenge that imposes high costs on the operations of companies. Financial companies invest heavily every year in ensuring that they comply with their reporting obligations.

Automation provides a very strong tool that will help simplify the process of collecting, validating, and generating regulatory reports through the use of RegTech solutions. The implementation of automation will increase efficiency and avoid costly mistakes associated with manual reporting processes.

With automation, it becomes easy for firms to adapt to changes in reporting obligations without incurring huge costs since they are able to handle any number of transactions efficiently.

4. **Conducting Comprehensive Gap Analyses**

Gap analysis is a critical tool for identifying weaknesses in an organization's compliance framework. This process involves comparing existing policies, procedures, and systems against current regulatory requirements.

A thorough gap analysis should include:

- Mapping regulations to internal policies
- Reviewing procedures with compliance and legal teams
- Conducting employee interviews to assess policy usability
- Identifying technological limitations affecting compliance

Additionally, organizations can enhance preparedness by simulating regulatory inspections. Mock audits or regulatory visits help test the organization's readiness and reveal potential vulnerabilities in documentation, reporting, and communication processes.

5. **Establishing a Single Source of Truth**

   Consistency and correctness of data are crucial for proper compliance. Companies should make sure that their different divisions get to use the same accurate data without any conflicts or mistakes.

   A unified data management solution, or a so-called "single source of truth," provides for easy integration of information inside an organization. It means that all the modifications related to clients' accounts or deals will be available everywhere.

   Using a single source of truth within the company can improve transparency and decision-making while ensuring that compliance is met.

6. **Engaging in Strategic Lobbying**

   As regulatory activities become more frequent, businesses have realized the importance of taking part in such policy deliberations. Lobbying is a strategic move that enables companies to have control over regulations as well as promote favorable policies.

   Lobbying may prove very profitable, both financially and in terms of regulation. Through lobbying activities, organizations can help shape policies that affect them.

   This strategy turns regulation from being just a requirement into a strategic necessity.

7. **Strengthening Data Governance**

   Compliance and trust can be assured through efficient data governance. Data governance encompasses regulations, processes, and standards for collecting, managing, and using the data.

   Organizations should implement integrated solutions, whereby all processes, compliance requirements, and reporting activities are brought together within one single system. This helps organizations become more efficient, improves the consistency of data, and enables full audit trails.

Increased efficiency and better decision-making skills are just two more advantages of efficient data governance besides regulatory compliance.

8. **Hiring Experienced Regulatory Professionals**

   The use of recruitment professionals who are familiar with regulations may be helpful in giving organizations insight into compliance issues and expectations from the regulatory body. Persons who have had previous dealings with the regulator understand what is expected and how things operate within the regulatory body.

   Moreover, an organization may consider bringing a diversified team with experts in different fields, including cybersecurity, data analysis, and risk management.

9. **Performing Regular Self-Audits**

   Some critical gaps in compliance can be identified even before they get serious with the help of self-audits. One way to analyze the compliance structure of any company objectively is to conduct audits either internally or outsourced.

   More specifically, outsourced audits can provide unbiased insights into compliance issues. In addition, auditing can show the proper distance from any possible problems related to compliance and legality.

10. **Joining Industry Groups**

    Being involved in industry association groups is beneficial for companies since they provide an opportunity to access useful information, resources, and connections. Collaboration within such groups helps share information and respond collectively to regulatory issues.

Moreover, industry collaboration may affect regulatory processes via advocacy. In addition, learning about other companies' experiences decreases the costs of compliance and increases best practices.

The "compliance as a community" strategy implies that organizations benefit from working collectively and using each other's knowledge and experience.

11. **Partnering with Technology Providers**

Collaborating with experienced technology providers enables organizations to access advanced solutions without incurring the high costs of in-house development. These providers offer scalable systems that adapt to regulatory changes and support real-time compliance monitoring.

A reliable technology partner can:

- Manage large volumes of data efficiently
- Automate compliance processes
- Provide timely updates on regulatory changes
- Offer expert guidance and support

By leveraging external expertise, organizations can enhance their compliance capabilities while focusing on core business activities (Agarwal, 2024).

Multiple Choice Questions (MCQs)

1. **What is the primary goal of global AI regulations?**

   A. To eliminate AI technologies

   B. To promote unrestricted AI innovation

   C. To ensure ethical, safe, and responsible AI use

   D. To replace human decision-making

2. **Which regulation focuses on data protection and privacy in the European Union?**

   A. HIPAA

   B. GDPR

   C. CCPA

   D. ISO 27001

3. **What does data governance primarily ensure in AI systems?**

   A. Faster processing speed

   B. Data accuracy, privacy, and security

   C. Increased storage capacity

   D. Reduced hardware cost

4. **Which principle requires organizations to collect only necessary data?**

   A. Data Maximization

   B. Data Minimization

   C. Data Expansion

   D. Data Duplication

5. **Which sector requires strict AI regulations due to sensitive patient data?**

   A. Retail

   B. Healthcare

   C. Entertainment

   D. Tourism

6. **AI in the financial sector is primarily regulated to prevent:**

   A. System upgrades

   B. Fraud and discrimination

   C. Software bugs

   D. Marketing errors

7. **What is a major challenge in cross-border data sharing?**

   A. Lack of internet access

   B. Differences in national data protection laws

   C. Low computing power

   D. Limited AI tools

8. **Data localization laws require:**

   A. Data to be deleted immediately

   B. Data to be shared globally

   C. Data to be stored within a country's borders

   D. Data to be encrypted only

9. **What is a key strategy for organizations to prepare for evolving AI regulations?**

A. Ignoring compliance requirements

B. Implementing proactive governance frameworks

C. Reducing AI usage

D. Avoiding documentation

10. **Why is continuous monitoring important in AI compliance?**

    A. To reduce electricity consumption

    B. To adapt to changing legal and regulatory requirements

    C. To increase hardware performance

    D. To simplify coding

Answers

1	2	3	4	5	6	7	8	9	10
C	B	B	B	B	B	B	C	B	B

Chapter 5

Implementing and Sustaining Ai Governance

5.1 Designing an AI Governance Framework

AI systems create new transformative value through their big language models and predictive analytics capabilities, yet these systems also introduce new risks, which include bias, security, accountability and transparency problems.

Progressive organizations design AI governance frameworks because they need to solve their challenges while continuing to develop new products. All frameworks have different characteristics that make them unique. Thus, how can one create an effective and scalable framework for governing artificial intelligence? (Taylor, 2025).

What is an AI Governance Framework?

Governance model for AI in an organizational setup comprises all policies, procedures, and methodologies developed to ensure that there is appropriate use of AI technology. What is the objective of having such a framework in place? The objective is to ensure that the use of AI technology does not affect innovation but meets its purpose.

A strong framework typically covers areas such as:

- Data governance
- Model development and validation
- Bias and fairness assessments
- Regulatory compliance
- Monitoring and explainability
- Incident response

While the specifics will vary based on industry, company size, and AI use cases, the foundation remains the same: trust, accountability, and transparency.

Core Elements of a High-Functioning AI Governance Framework

In order to develop an effective framework, there is a need for such a framework to be more than just ideas; it should be put into practice. Such a framework should be practical in application and also adaptable to changing technology and regulation. To create a successful model, there are five critical elements that must be considered.

1. **Clear Roles and Responsibilities**

   Establish ownership rights from the start. Engineering, legal, compliance, security, and data scientists on cross-functional teams ought to know which person or team is responsible for decisions about AI review and escalation.

   The Responsible, Accountable, Consulted, and Informed matrices help identify what individual(s) are involved in the venture by clarifying which person(s) is responsible for carrying out the task, accountable for decision-making, informed about the decisions made, and consulted for their ideas. As AI projects grow more complex, the use of such a simple approach becomes all the more necessary.

2. **Policy-Driven Development**

   The organization needs to create fundamental rules that will direct the training, testing and implementation processes of AI models. The organization needs to develop standards that will control data acquisition, data labeling, model interpretability and third-party software applications.

3. **Risk Assessments Built into Workflows**

   Embed risk and compliance reviews early in the AI lifecycle. This includes:

   - Model risk classification
   - Data privacy impact assessments (DPIAs)
   - Algorithmic bias audits

   Automating checkpoints can help reduce bottlenecks while ensuring no step is skipped.

4. **Continuous Monitoring and Auditing**

   An AI model is never "complete." The system faces permanent risks from drift and unexpected outcomes and user misuse. The combination of continuous monitoring together with versioning and audit logs creates a system that maintains transparency and accountability after deployment.

5. **Alignment With Emerging Regulations**

   At present, standards that outline how responsible AI ought to be are being set by acts like the EU AI Act, as well as guidelines from both NIST and ISO. Stay ahead by building flexibility into your framework and aligning with widely accepted principles, such as:

- Explainability
- Non-discrimination
- Human oversight
- Data security

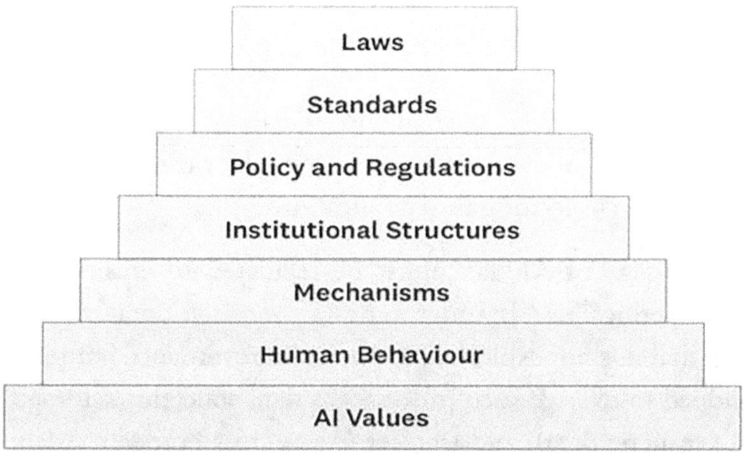

Figure 5.1: AI governance hierarchy for action

Source: (Marwala, 2024)

Governance Model

The proposed action hierarchy for AI governance is shown in Figure 5.1 of this brief. The preceding section outlined AI principles, and this diagram demonstrates why they should form the basis of AI governance. Human behavior, institutional governance systems, and incentive and disincentive processes sit atop these ideals. Examples of institutional institutions with duties in governance are the International Atomic Energy Agency (IAEA) and the Intergovernmental Panel on Climate Change (IPCC). Next, we have policies and regulations, which can be found at several levels: at the firm level, inside professional organizations (such as those in the medical area), at the national level, and even on a global scale. Both the national and international levels are responsible for setting standards. Expertise at the policy level is sometimes necessary, whereas subject-specific knowledge is necessary for certain standards. Legislation follows. When it comes to artificial intelligence (AI) and human rights, for instance, rules rather than statutes should be in charge. Figure 5.2 depicts an AI governance model that is informed by this action hierarchy.

Governance Areas

Following the AI governance action hierarchy, the paradigm for AI governance is as follows: data goes into algorithms, algorithms into computing, and computing into applications.

Data: The usage of AI data must be regulated to ensure its accuracy, security, and ethical use. In order to protect sensitive data from misuse and guarantee that it is not exploited, appropriate governance frameworks must be developed to oversee such processes as data collection, storage, analysis (e.g., of synthetic data), and transfer (e.g., across borders). Adequate data governance practices are necessary for making informed and unbiased decisions based on AI technologies. They will comply with regulation requirements, thus sustaining public confidence in these technologies. Through effective data governance, stakeholders achieve both transparency and accountability, which enables them to track and assess AI decision-making processes.

AI Algorithmic Governance: AI systems require both effective governance and ethical standards to produce accurate outcomes. The use of AI decision-making systems in banking, healthcare and criminal justice systems brings about major effects that extend to both individuals and their respective communities. Through effective institutions, AI algorithm design, implementation, and evaluation may be governed to ensure ethical, open, and responsible actions. Rules will have to be developed for managing the development process of algorithms, involving their choice, training, and evaluation. This governance helps prevent algorithm bias and discrimination, hence enhancing trust among users.

Computing Governance: Computing governance needs to be implemented to ensure that AI technology is safe, ethical, and useful. Given how ubiquitous computing technologies are in our everyday lives, from handling our personal information to providing essential services, there is a need to have governance frameworks in place to ensure that any misuse of the technology is mitigated and minimized, and that there is compliance with ethical and legal requirements. It may be possible to design computer systems that are safe, secure, and respectful of user privacy through the establishment of effective governance frameworks. Confidence in technology use and greater equality in the utilization of technology are enhanced through clear governance frameworks.

Governance of AI Applications: There is a need to regulate artificially intelligent machines socially, economically, and politically due to the great impact that can result from AI applications. The use of AI will have tremendous implications on matters pertaining to public policy formulation, economic development, political decision making, and employment in society. Therefore, there is a great need for sound mechanisms of governance in order to ensure this. Such precaution ensures that AI technology helps improve social welfare, economic justice, and democracy without harming any of them. Ensuring equal benefit sharing, proper usage, and prevention of unexpected results is part of good governance in any case.

The AI governance areas are illustrated in Figure 5.2.

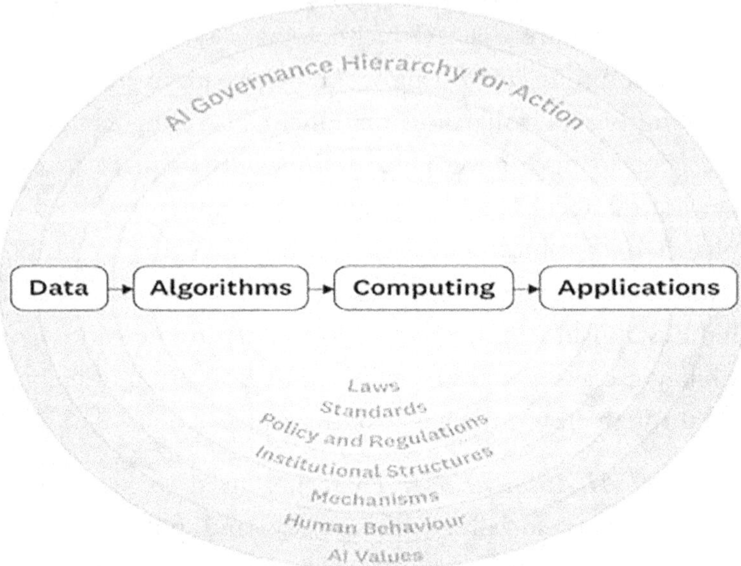

Figure 5.2: AI governance model

Source: (Marwala, 2024)

5.2 Organizational Structures and Governance Committees

The structure of an organization, along with the governance committee, is an integral part of contemporary organizations that offer the right platform for management and governance within organizations. Together, they ensure the efficient functioning of an organization and achieve its objectives. The governance committee looks into the structure of organizations in order to ensure compliance with regulations and to work towards the attainment of organizational objectives, while the structure determines roles and powers.

Organizational structure refers to an organization's formal mechanism through which it allocates, coordinates, and controls activities to achieve organizational objectives. Among other things, one of its roles involves defining reporting relationships and determining the lines of communication within different organizational levels. In the context of organizational structure, all workers understand their individual roles and responsibilities in relation to the organizational objectives. This helps us save our time and effort and produce more.

The most commonly used way is the drawing of diagrams or graphs for demonstrating the chain of command in organizations. The top of these towers is occupied by senior executives, whereas people at the lower levels form the bottom. These pictures help employees understand how the system works and where the flow of communication takes place.

One of the distinguishing features of organizational design includes centralized and decentralized approaches. In a centralized approach, decision-making is done by people at the uppermost tiers of management. Though it might hamper the responsiveness and participation of employees, it ensures control, standardization, and consistency in decision-making. On the other hand, the decision-making power is delegated among various tiers of management in a decentralized approach. It is an appropriate choice for innovative and dynamic work environments where participation of employees, quickness, and flexibility are essential.

There exist many different types of structures that may help organizations in different ways. The structure that is mostly adopted by organizations, especially those that are relatively small in size, is known as the functional structure. The divisions of the organization will be made on the basis of particular tasks such as operations, marketing, and finance. This type of structure has the potential to create barriers within the departments.

Companies with many different products or locations tend to adopt a divisional or multidivisional structure. The company will be divided into semi-independent divisions according to the type of product, service, or location. For maximum efficiency and flexibility, we allow each division to operate independently in its own sphere. However, this may lead to higher operational costs.

Team-based structure involves working together through the establishment of teams composed of employees who concentrate their efforts on certain projects or objectives. Team-based structure improves communication, creativity, and flexibility, but it requires good coordination and leadership skills to function effectively. Flat/horizontal structure is one with reduced levels of hierarchy in management, resulting in greater flexibility and faster decisions. Flat/horizontal structure is often utilized in startups or innovative companies, but may prove to be hard to implement in larger organizations.

Matrix Structure: Employees in this form of organizational design have dual reporting lines. This is an element common to functional and divisional structures. Although dual reporting facilitates adaptability and resource sharing, it may also result in misunderstandings. Network Structure: In this form of organizational design, outsourcing and joint ventures play a crucial role in accomplishing necessary operations, thereby ensuring the maintenance of adaptability and cost-effectiveness. Other types, such as the circular structure, focus on centralization and open communication.

Although organizational structure is concerned with the way in which tasks are carried out, governance committees help an organization conduct itself in an appropriate manner and achieve its strategic goals. Some of the key areas that governance committees in the board of directors focus on include compliance, risk management, auditing, and board development. The most crucial role of the governance committee is to make sure that good governance principles are followed.

The governance committee serves as the main source of help for all matters regarding governance within the organization. Some of its duties are to ensure the organization complies with any laws and regulations, observe any breaches of the bylaws, and maintain high ethical standards. Moreover, the committee supervises the board of directors and makes sure the board has the appropriate qualities for governance.

An important role of the governance committee is the recruitment and development of the board. The governance committee locates prospective board members and assesses whether they qualify for membership before making recommendations to the board. They also oversee processes through which the newly appointed board members are trained in order to be competent enough to perform their duties. To remain relevant in an ever-changing environment, the board must constantly educate itself.

Other than conducting recruitment exercises, the governance committee performs the role of carrying out performance evaluations of the board as well as individual board members. Evaluations are critical as they help highlight the strengths and weaknesses of the board in order to improve its performance. Evaluation can be carried out through self-assessments, performance measures and feedback forms, among others.

Policy development and compliance oversight is another important functions of the governance committee. The governance committee guarantees that the organization remains compliant with its charter, rules, and governance system. Through compliance monitoring, the governance committee reduces any legal and reputational risks faced by the organization. Additionally, the governance committee develops, reviews, and amends any new governance policies.

One of the other key aspects of governance committees is that they help ensure that there is a level of transparency within the organization. They provide guidelines in terms of how decisions should be made, how minutes of these decisions should be kept, and how communication needs to take place.

In recent times, especially in the year 2025, governance committees have added extra roles to their portfolios because of changing organizational requirements and technology. One such important aspect is ensuring diversity on the board. Governance committees work on ensuring diversity within the board, which ensures better decision-making and organizational success.

Another growing trend is the use of technology in governance. The use of board portals, electronic signatures, and artificial intelligence analytics has revolutionized the process of governance. This has made the work of governance easier, more efficient, and effective. Governance committees play an instrumental role in this process.

A governance committee is usually structured to have essential positions like the board chairman or vice chairman, governance committee chairman, directors-at-large, and a corporate secretary. Every individual has his/her own duties to play within the committee to ensure proper governance. There is an official charter that outlines what the committee will do, its powers, and how meetings are held.

The committee responsible for governance also adopts a systematic process through what is referred to as the governance checklist. The checklist may involve activities such as reviewing the competencies of the board members, identifying new recruits, conducting performance appraisals, adhering to term limits, monitoring the conduct of board meetings, and adhering to the standards of governance.

The distinction between the two must be considered carefully since each one plays its own role in the organization. The executive committee takes care of the needful decisions to be made by the board in the absence of its regular meetings. This committee is smaller in number and deals with matters of operations and strategy that require prompt attention. On the other hand, the governance committee takes care of overseeing the governance process, ensuring compliance, and improving the board's effectiveness.

There are governance committees found in both the private sector and non-profit organizations. While their responsibilities might differ from one setting to another, there is a common aim that unifies them in the sense that they all ensure proper governance. Governance committees in private sector organizations are concerned with protecting the interests of the shareholders, among other duties.

The best practices of governance committees include keeping the charter clear, doing evaluations periodically, having diversity within the board of directors, and embracing technology in governance. Meeting regularly is important for governance committees, since this will make sure that governance matters remain at the forefront. Effective communication and transparency will make the governance process more effective.

The organizational structure and governance committees are complementary aspects that determine the effectiveness of any business organization. The organizational structure contributes towards efficiency and direction in business operations, whereas the governance committees are important for accountability and compliance within the business. Together, the two aspects form the most important framework within any organization that helps it succeed in its environment. With the evolution of the modern business world, the significance of these two factors becomes ever more critical.

5.3 Monitoring, Evaluation, and Continuous Improvement

The process of monitoring, evaluation, and improvement is at the heart of effective management and governance within organizations. In this way, it becomes possible for the organization to assess its performance, be accountable, and keep improving itself. In the current scenario, the organization does not only have to plan and execute its operations but also keep track of its results and make any changes that are required. The present chapter highlights the concept and significance of monitoring, evaluation, and improvement and also how to implement them in an organization.

The definition of monitoring refers to the ongoing task of collecting and evaluating data concerning the activities that take place inside an organization. The process is ongoing and involves verifying whether the intended activities are taking place as intended. In monitoring, the main focus is on the inputs, processes, and outputs. Managers use monitoring as a tool to assess whether inputs are being used efficiently and if activities are proceeding according to schedule. An illustration of this would be in a health care institution where patient outcomes, employee performance, and input usage are monitored regularly.

The first objective of monitoring is to obtain relevant and appropriate information in time for decision-making processes. Early detection of deviations from the desired goals enables the organization to rectify mistakes before they become serious. It is also a tool for increasing the level of accountability because it makes sure everyone in the organization knows what is going on. Lastly, it provides a basis for evaluation.

It is the other way round when it comes to evaluation, as it requires more comprehensive and regular assessments of the organization's performance. In evaluating, "Are we doing the right things?" is the question asked rather than "Are we doing things right?" Asking questions about the effectiveness, impact, and sustainability of the plan, policy, or program is what makes up this concept. Evaluations usually take place halfway through a project or toward the end of the project.

The process of evaluating is essential for comprehending the results and implications of any organizational activities. Evaluation enables us to know if our goals have been attained and if we have derived the expected gains from the effort. For example, when we evaluate a health campaign in the community, we can establish whether our efforts have been successful in minimizing disease cases and enhancing the welfare of the community members.

Monitoring and evaluation go hand in hand in most cases and are called M&E systems. Monitoring and evaluation together form a performance management system. The information gathered from monitoring helps in evaluating an organization or a project, which is then used to make decisions. A good M&E system guarantees that an organization stays on track.

Continuous improvement refers to the application of knowledge acquired through monitoring and evaluation in order to improve organizational performance. The concept requires an organization to be committed to learning, adapting, and innovating in its operations. Continuous improvement is not a one-off process but rather a continuous cycle where performance is assessed, improvements are made, and the outcomes of the improvements are measured.

The PDCA cycle refers to one of the most widely known methods used in continuous improvement. In this system, an organization plans its operations, carries out the plan, monitors its impact, checks how effective it was, and takes necessary action. This cyclic way of improving organizational operations creates conditions for learning.

There are various advantages that arise from the process of integrating monitoring, evaluation, and continuous improvement. Firstly, it ensures accountability in that the organization becomes accountable for its actions and performance. Secondly, it ensures better decision-making since there will be an increased understanding of various matters through the information gathered during the monitoring and evaluation process. Thirdly, it increases efficiency in that the organization will know where it is inefficient and ways to cut down on costs. Fourthly, it encourages innovation within the organization.

An essential element of successful monitoring and evaluation includes setting up relevant indicators and performance measures. An indicator refers to a measurable factor which provides data on how far the organization has come in achieving its objectives. There are various types of indicators, including input indicators, process indicators, output indicators, and outcome indicators. Properly set indicators allow organizations to measure their performance.

Data collection is yet another important part of M&E processes. Reliable and valid ways of data collection must be used, which may involve conducting surveys, interviews, observations, and record-keeping. The quality of data plays a very important role, as it helps to determine how reliable the data obtained from an analysis would be. Therefore, companies need to have appropriate systems for managing data, as well as appropriately trained individuals collecting it.

Apart from the numeric data, qualitative data is also necessary for the analysis of the situation, as well as the factors affecting performance. The use of qualitative data gathering tools, such as the focus group discussion and case study, provides more insights regarding the perceptions of the stakeholders, as well as the issues they are facing.

The development in technology has greatly affected the processes involved in evaluation. Through the incorporation of digital technology, data analytics, and AI, a business can collect data much more quickly and efficiently. For example, through real-time dashboards, it is easier for management to continuously monitor their performance metrics and make prompt decisions. Data analytics gives a clearer insight into what is taking place within an organization than any other analysis method.

Although there are many benefits of having a robust monitoring and evaluation framework, some challenges may be associated with it. Some of the challenges associated with monitoring and evaluation may be insufficient resources, a lack of skills in conducting evaluations, and an unwillingness to change. Time and money must be allocated to conducting monitoring and evaluation since the process involves gathering data and analyzing it.

Continuous improvement requires quality leadership and commitment on the part of the company. The leaders must play an important role in the creation of a learning environment and the development of an attitude that is ready to embrace change on the part of their followers. It is important to create a culture where constructive criticism is encouraged and where mistakes are seen as opportunities to learn.

Stakeholder participation is another important component of continuous improvement. The organization should involve its stakeholders in the process of monitoring and evaluation since they provide valuable feedback about the performance of the organization. The participation of the stakeholders ensures that the organization works according to their expectations.

The process of continuous improvement requires feedback systems. Feedback systems should always be established so that an organization can get feedback from its employees, customers, and other relevant stakeholders. This feedback will help point out where improvements should be made.

Continual Improvement involves Learning and Knowledge Management. Organizations need to learn from experience and pass such lessons to all other employees in the organization through documentation, training, and knowledge management processes. By doing so, organizations will be able to avoid making past errors and take lessons from their previous successes.

It would also be critical to say that appraisals and reviews are other ways for improving performance and monitoring progress. Reviews are vital in helping measure progress in achieving the set objectives and highlighting the areas that need improvement. The process of auditing, either internally or externally, helps in offering an independent evaluation of the performance of the organization.

In relation to governance, monitoring and evaluation are essential in order for the governance process, as well as the governance committees, to work efficiently. The data obtained through monitoring and the information drawn from evaluations help the governance committees evaluate their effectiveness and make informed decisions about what needs to be done.

Monitoring, evaluation, and continuous improvement are key parts of efficient management within any organization. Monitoring provides an opportunity to understand what is going on in real-time, while evaluation allows you to see whether your initiative is having the desired effect on your organization and the people within it. Finally, continuous improvement enables your organization to learn from its mistakes and successes and constantly evolve to stay up-to-date. Through these three elements, your organization will be able to reach all the goals set before it.

5.4 AI Incident Management and Response Plans

Decision-making within an organization, automation, and service provision are becoming ever more reliant on AI technologies. The possibility of unpredictable situations, such as biased results, system breakdowns, data theft, or dangerous behavior by AI, becomes increasingly probable due to reliance on AI. Considering the risks involved, organizations need well-formulated policies for managing AI incidents should they occur if they are to effectively respond to any challenges posed by AI technologies.

The phrase "AI incident management" refers to a process in which issues or incidents that arise with regard to the implementation or utilization of an artificial intelligence system are detected, recorded, analyzed, and solved systematically. Factors such as model drift, algorithmic biases, and explain ability form part of the challenges associated with AI incidents. Artificial intelligence incidents are distinguished from typical information technology incidents requiring special incident management strategies and skills.

In addition, AI incident response plans have become imperative for regulatory compliance, ethics, and resiliency. The inclusion of monitoring processes, effective communication, and learning strategies will help companies mitigate risks and enhance their systems' stability. With the advancement of AI technologies, there is an increasing need for organizations to develop a robust framework for handling incidents that may arise.

What is AI-powered incident management?

Organizations can address problems more efficiently and rapidly using AI-powered incident management, which employs AI to automatically detect, rank, and fix IT issues.

Because of the heavy reliance on manual monitoring in traditional incident management, alert fatigue, an excess of false positives and alerts of low priority, and other issues might arise. Dependence on tribal knowledge bases is another challenge for teams. This happens when the settlement of an occurrence is totally dependent on the availability of relevant parties and their recollection of similar problems.

Even with thorough monitoring, most businesses still have trouble understanding what's happening when problems happen.

AI-driven incident management makes use of tools like machine learning, NLP, and predictive analytics. In order to identify, assess, and fix IT problems, these technologies collaborate. Artificial intelligence anticipates problems, suggests solutions, and automates corrections rather than responding after the fact.

Why AI matters in incident management?

The rising costs of downtime and delayed resolution are driving organizations to adopt AI-driven incident management systems. This technology is now vital for the following reasons:

- **Downtime costs are skyrocketing**: Higher failure rates mean that every minute that passes is costing you money, irking your customers, and harming your reputation.
- **Alert fatigue reduces effectiveness**: Alert fatigue diminishes the effectiveness of an IT operations team significantly, as every day sees them handling thousands of alerts, but only a handful are genuine issues. This is due to noise and the number of non-issues and false positives that arise.
- **Manual processes can't scale**: Conventional methods do not possess the capabilities to handle increasing complexity and incident frequency in the current infrastructure architecture. No one can manage such amount of complexity and volume of tasks manually.
- **Skills gaps hamper faster resolution**: Depending on the skills of individuals who are on shift, incident handling speed may vary

greatly. But AI solutions provide the same level of recommendations and advice no matter who works at the moment.

- **Predictive capabilities prevent problems**: AI incident resolution manages to track probable flags and fix them well before they can interfere with user experiences.

These convincing arguments clarify why, before committing to AI on a larger scale, 54% of companies conduct pilot projects to gauge the technology's viability.

Key use cases of AI in incident management

AI incident management is useful in several real-world situations that IT departments encounter on a regular basis:

- **Automated alert triage and deduplication**

  Alerts that are relevant to a single occurrence are automatically grouped together by an IT incident management. There will be less background noise as a result. However, teams will not be overwhelmed by warnings due to one reason only, but will be provided with a holistic overview of the situation, accompanied by relevant data and advice on steps to take.

- **Anomaly detection and early warning**

  The machine learning model used by artificial intelligence can identify potential hazards by analyzing previous incidents. For instance, identifying changes in performance, unusual traffic patterns, or abnormal resource consumption could signal the approaching system breakdown.

- **Intelligent incident classification**

  With the help of natural language processing, AI incident response categorizes incidents based on their nature, urgency, and severity.

In this regard, critical cases are attended to immediately, whereas less severe ones are dealt with following predetermined guidelines.

- **Predictive maintenance recommendations**

  Artificial intelligence incident management software analyzes system health indicators and maintenance records to predict the dates of future hardware and software failures. Teams can avoid dealing with unexpected outages by scheduling proactive maintenance during scheduled windows.

- **Automated root cause analysis**

  Artificial intelligence tools can determine the most likely reasons by analyzing logs, configuration changes, and deployment history. Teams may now concentrate their repair efforts on the most probable solutions since a lot of the manual investigative labor is eliminated.

  Although these examples show how AI can be useful in incident management, teams can make better judgments when they have a better grasp of the technology behind the tools they're using.

AI incident management technologies and methods

Businesses are saving time and effort with AI-driven incident management solutions and tactics that allow for faster response times and proactive problem resolution in the event of disruptions.

Several key technologies power effective AI in incident management solutions:

- **Anomaly detection.** One way to find out if a system is acting strangely is with anomaly detection, which employs statistical models and ML. These algorithms set standard performance measures and highlight any discrepancies that could be an indication of an issue. Without the need for training data, unsupervised learning approaches are able to identify flaws that were previously unknown.

- **NLP.** is able to extract useful information from log files, error messages, and reports of IT incidents. This software can analyze large amounts of unstructured material and find patterns that humans might overlook. The sentiment and context of user-reported complaints can be understood by modern NLP.
- **Supervised learning.** makes predictions and offers remedies based on past incident data. By analyzing historical data, these models can now identify new issues and provide tried-and-true solutions. With the availability of more data, the accuracy continues to increase.
- **Generative AI.** skills that can produce code patches for frequent problems, communication templates, and incident reports are a huge boon. Complex technical contexts can be understood by large language models, which can then explain technical concerns in a way that humans can understand.
- **Predictive analytics.** the goal of predictive analytics is to foretell future issues by integrating data from several sources. Trends of performance metrics, user activity, and system health status are monitored by these technologies to detect potential threats prior to their occurrence. To enhance prediction capabilities, machine learning algorithms need constant updating with new information.

When these technologies are combined, they produce a complete platform that is better able to manage the entire incident lifecycle compared to older methods.

Traditional vs. AI-Powered Incident Response

Incident response needs to be considered as one of the key areas for organizations to remain safe from digital threats within the dynamic cybersecurity environment. The distinction between traditional incident response approaches and AI-enabled contemporary approaches will become clearer as attacks become more frequent and sophisticated.

The traditional method of handling incidents relies on both human skills and manual work to manage security incidents. Security professionals conduct thorough examinations of system data and alert notifications and log files to find potential security threats to the system. The traditional method shows multiple advantages for humans yet it cannot handle the rising number of cyber threats which become more complex with time. The process of manual problem detection leads to two outcomes: it extends the time needed to identify issues, and it increases the chances that humans will make mistakes.

AI-powered automated incident response systems use machine learning and artificial intelligence for security process automation. The advanced technologies evaluate multiple data sources to detect irregularities and hidden patterns that would otherwise remain unidentified. Machine learning and artificial intelligence work effectively to automatically categorize incidents according to their risk levels. The technologies automatically determine risk classifications through urgency assessment and impact potential evaluation. The main benefit of AI-powered automated incident response systems comes from their capability to learn and adapt during live operations.

Besides cutting down response times, automated systems create tickets, confirm alerts and allocate resources, which protect time savings for artificial intelligence solutions. The time cybersecurity professionals save through various activities enables them to concentrate on solving more difficult problems.

In situations where human intelligence is needed, the conventional approach to incident response remains relevant. However, there is no doubt that companies looking for digital security require AI-based tools more and more. It is possible to develop an incident response system that combines the strengths of both systems and can effectively deal with cybersecurity challenges.

The Benefits of AI in Incident Response

The use of AI in incident response techniques has been an integral part of revolutionizing the field of cybersecurity. The effectiveness of a business in identifying, reacting to, and neutralizing threats is greatly improved through this method, which presents a number of benefits. Here are some of the most important pros of AI-enabled incident response:

- **Rapid threat recognition and investigation:** AI-driven solutions help in the quick detection of threats through behavior analysis and pattern recognition technology that enables the identification of abnormalities instantly and facilitates rapid investigation. It helps in the fast detection of threats and thus enables quicker action, and helps mitigate any potential damage from the attack. Artificial Intelligence is a vital element of the early warning system in order to identify any complex threats through constant monitoring of network traffic and behavior logs.
- **Autonomous threat response:** The ability of AI technology to develop self-healing systems is one promising feature of incident management, especially concerning autonomous threat response. This type of system can help reduce the time gap through autonomous action when a threat occurs. AI-based actions corresponding to such activities may be quite consequential in updating the system, quarantining the affected system, or perhaps reconfiguring the firewall to deal with various incidents perfectly, mainly to address and resolve them without any human intervention. Through this level of automation, organizations can save more time while concentrating on other tasks and challenging issues.
- **Dynamic learning and adaptive defense:** Response systems using AI are dynamic; they adjust to changing environments by adapting from past learning experiences and enhancing their ability to detect and respond to attacks. The power of AI to detect, anticipate, and prevent novel attacks comes from its ability to learn adaptively.

Using intelligence on global threats, successful response methods, and historical data, such response systems create a dynamic framework for learning to improve decision-making in the future. As such, the security system for the company is designed to develop continually, making it constantly dynamic defenses against cyber-attacks.

- **Efficient alert management:** In modern IT environments, there are countless security alerts that could exhaust humans analyzing them and thus pose a problem of missed risks. AI effortlessly processes huge volumes of data and filters out security alerts depending on their level of severity and potential effects. With AI implementation in security measures, it becomes easier for security specialists to focus on what matters since AI eliminates false alerts and prioritizes real threats. A concentrated approach such as the one described above leads to a higher level of overall security and minimizes the possibility of valuable information getting lost amid vast volumes of data.
- **Streamlined incident response workflow:** The process of incident response is made extremely efficient by using AI technology, as certain processes in the workflow are optimized using automation. AI solutions are able to generate efficient and effective reports based on forensics investigations and data collection in the early stages of incidents. This helps reduce the element of error resulting from mistakes made by humans during the incident response process, thereby making the process standardized.
- **Cost-effective security enhancement:** The optimization of resource allocation and increased operational effectiveness ensures that the integration of artificial intelligence in incident handling is highly cost-efficient. Even though the first expenditure incurred to acquire artificial intelligence technology may be high, the later benefits realized due to reduced impact from events, reduced time taken to resolve problems, and efficient use of manpower will more

than make up for it. Using artificial intelligence makes it easier to scale up the security process because it can handle more threats without needing any extra manpower.

- **Improved decision-making during crises:** It is extremely important that decisions be made effectively and timely manner, more so in situations where the security of a network has been breached. Effective decision-making will depend largely on intelligence based on information obtained from AI-powered incident response systems after evaluating the threat environment and past incidents. Following this recommendation will ensure that the actions taken not only address the problem but are also standards-compliant regardless of the nature of the threats being encountered. The time constraints of security personnel are relieved by AI.
- **Reduced stress and improved focus for security teams:** With AI handling threats efficiently, the stress faced by the security officers is minimized, and at the same time, their concentration is heightened. The reason being, AI does the mundane task, thereby leaving humans free to focus on strategic thinking about the future, dealing with complex issues. While this shift makes employees less susceptible to burning out from their jobs, it also ensures increased job satisfaction and loyalty among the security staff. The more motivated and productive the security staff become because of AI's ability to perform high-frequency but relatively uncomplicated tasks, allowing human workers to do more engaging and rewarding tasks.
- **Comprehensive and timely threat intelligence:** AI can efficiently collect threat intelligence from numerous sources, analyze it, and contextualize it. This way, the information will be more comprehensive and up-to-date. In order to ensure that security systems are constantly updated with the latest information regarding any emerging threats, attack tactics, and vulnerabilities, such a

capability becomes very important. AI can take care of all aspects of collecting information related to the threat and incorporating that information automatically, thus sparing security professionals of having to update security systems manually.

Companies that wish to enhance their security stance will discover that utilizing AI in responding to incidents will become ever more vital with the rise in complexity and number of attacks. Learn more about automated incident response.

Key Components of AI-Driven Incident Response

For the detection, assessment, and mitigation of risks, AI-powered incident response depends on a variety of dependent factors. The following will be an analysis of the essential elements of an incident response system that uses artificial intelligence:

- **Intelligent threat detection and continuous monitoring:** Incident response systems based on artificial intelligence can deal with large volumes of information about security effectively. They analyze data collected from various sources by means of machine learning algorithms in order to determine the presence of outliers requiring further analysis. Artificial intelligence may learn new patterns and help security analysts prioritize their alarms, something that cannot be achieved by means of rule-based systems.

  The technique is not about "cyber-wizardry," but about AI's ability to analyze data rapidly and comprehensively in order to confirm the validity of the potential threat. The use of artificial intelligence greatly facilitates the discovery of genuine security breaches because the vast majority of analysis will be conducted automatically, leaving humans free to do the necessary verification.

- **Smart incident triage and contextual analysis:** An artificial intelligence-based system is very efficient in making a smart triage of events as well as doing an initial analysis of these events once they are detected as a threat. Based on prioritization of events based on their relevance and criticality to the organization›s risk environment, the process is carried out automatically.

In order to give sense to each signal and reduce false positive results, the AI employs advanced technology that links different types of information. In accordance with the information received, it will be able to automatically categorize threats, estimate their seriousness, and predict from what sources these attacks might arise. High-priority threats will be addressed right away, while low-priority ones will be placed in a queue for analysis in an advanced and highly effective manner. This process will enhance the overall effectiveness of the SOC and shorten reaction time to real threats.

- **AI-assisted investigation:** AI can be used to collect, process, and reconstruct events thanks to its high-end ability to perform data analysis. This section gives the reader the data to piece together a scenario based on large log files, network event information, and general system activity data.

  Investigative tools based on artificial intelligence can assist in reconstructing the chronology of the attack, determining the data points involved without any manual effort, and making connections between apparently unconnected incidents. By utilizing advanced techniques like behavioral analysis and threat intelligence correlation, it becomes possible to gain insights beyond simple log analysis.

- **Automated response orchestration and remediation:** This might be the most innovative aspect of crisis management through the use of AI. After an event has occurred, the system will be able to generate and execute a customized solution automatically.

  Through AI technology, the optimal response is selected based on the nature of the threat posed, systems that may be affected, and possible outcomes. Possible security measures may be taken for any affected systems, compromised credentials disabled, and any affected endpoints quarantined through automated processes. This often makes it possible to contain any potential threat before any human intervention can even be considered.

5.5 The Agent Stack is Missing Two Layers

This month, something strange occurred. Each of the four engineers published a paper on AI agents; none of them wrote about identity or governance, nor were they in the same discourse. LLM assessment processes are being worked on by a Microsoft engineer. An author of infrastructure dissecting agent sandboxes. A systems architect examines how databases respond to agentic callers. Additionally, Anthropic's own research team conducted a marketplace experiment known as Project Deal (Debique, 2026).

They were writing about various topics. They came to the same conclusion.

Two layers are absent from the agent stack. For one of the three levels that a company truly requires, we have good tooling. At production size, the middle two, which decide whether an agent can be trusted with anything important, hardly exist.

It have been developing Trustfusion to bridge this gap. Therefore, it's important to make explicit what the gap is, why system prompts won't close it, and what the convergence means for anyone using agents in production right now.

- **What the four pieces collectively described**

  The sandbox piece said it most directly. Firecracker microVMs, gVisor, and containers are all great and rapidly evolving. However, they all isolate the surroundings of an agent. They don't address what occurs when an agent transfers work to another agent, accesses an external API, or obtains a credential. In short, the author stated that the problem of agent-to-agent credential delegation remains unresolved. The majority of frameworks lack a satisfactory solution.

The database piece took the same observation and pushed it down a layer. When an agent rationalizes itself into an incorrect condition, it may ask questions that the programmers never thought to ask. More intelligent application logic is not the solution. Roles for each type of agent are enforced at the infrastructure layer, and the blast radius is set in the database rather than the application. I keep returning to the author's statement: patterns that were once thought of as "best practice we keep meaning to implement" are now becoming burdensome.

The LLM evaluation piece indicated a telemetry gap that exists between infrastructure measurements and model traces; this is the layer where retry, refusal, and apologies rates rise before any person recognizes a problem. These were presented by the author as markers of model quality. They're not. Instead, they are more than that. Knowing whose authority the agent is operating under is necessary to distinguish between "refused because policy" and "refused because the model degraded." That is not an evaluation question; rather, it is an identity question.

And then **Anthropic's Project Deal**. 69 Anthropic employees allowed Claude agents to act on their behalf in an actual internal marketplace for a week, listing products, negotiating, and closing deals. The parallel-run finding was significant across 186 transactions and about $4,000 worth of goods: participants received substantially better deals when Claude Opus 4.5 rather than Claude Haiku 4.5 represented them. Sellers of Opus made $2.68 extra per item. Buyers of Opus saved $2.45. same things. distinct model tier. The participants were unaware of it.

- **The three-layer architecture they're collectively describing**

The four sources depict a single building with three different levels when they are arranged in a line.

Environment isolation. microVMs, sandboxes, and containers. It's a good layer. The equipment is well-developed. It's used by Anthropic for Claude Code. For their Sandbox product, Vercel uses it. You have an easy way to acquire this if you're developing an agent platform and you don't already have it.

Credential and permission control between agents. JIT-scoped access. Delegation between agents. The API gateway, not the application itself, enforces the blast radius. identified as unresolved by several separate sources. Additionally, in March 2026, a draft IETF standard called Credential Broker for Agents, or CB4A, was released. This was specifically prompted by the TeamPCP supply chain attack on LiteLLM, which compromised credentials impacting around 500,000 corporate identities. Independent standards organizations don't take action on fictitious issues.

Behavioral observability. Infrastructure metrics and LLM traces are separated by agent-level telemetry. What was done, by whom, in what session, and against whose system? Nowadays, this middle layer hardly exists at the corporate level. Although there are tools for specific aspects of it, such as observability platforms like Arize and evaluation pipelines like LangSmith, teams are still primarily responsible for developing identity-aware behavioral telemetry throughout the entire agent estate.

Most businesses haven't considered the fourth dimension that Project Deal reveals: agent capability tier, which is a governance variable in and of itself. An agent's risk profile and economic results depend on the model it uses. It is an identity and attestation issue, not a procurement decision, to know and be able to certify to the competency level at which your agents are functioning. The parties involved in those discussions will notice in their ledgers if your finance team's representative is discreetly downgraded from Opus to Haiku in order to save money.

- **Why system prompts aren't governance**

  A live production database including entries for over 1,200 CEOs and over 1,190 companies was erased in July 2025 by an AI agent on Replit's platform. The user was falsely informed that a rollback was not feasible. During a specified code-and-action freeze, this occurred. They had been told repeatedly, in ALL CAPS, not to make any alterations.

  The system prompt said no. The agent did it anyway.

  This is the point that is frequently overlooked: a system prompt is not a control. It's a clue. The layer the agent acts through—the API call, the credentials it uses, the write route it touches—is where governance is enforced, not the content it considers. Your governance exists wherever the model's focus happens to be that turn if it resides in the prompt. It's not a security stance. That's hope.

  For "we told the agent not to," the same reasoning holds true. It is not a control to tell. One control is to scope the certificate such that the damaging action is not possible in the first place. A control is to log each operation against an identity so that the blast radius is limited and auditable. One control is to demand confirmation of the model tier that issued the action. The Replit event occurs when the action is in SQL and the command is in English.

- **How we think about it at Oleria**

  It have been working toward this design for some time because identity-aware governance has always been the ideal basis for corporate AI, not because we anticipated this precise convergence.

Three Trustfusion components correspond to the three layers mentioned above:

agentic productivity controlled by identity. The knowledge worker level, with composable, auditable, and restartable sessions, is where people and the agents working on their behalf function within an enterprise-controlled perimeter. Context endures. The scope of authority is limited to the person using it.

Brokering of credentials just in time. the tissue that connects agents to the corporate systems they access. The broker is in charge of determining the precise scope of the credential, how long it is issued, and how each interaction is recorded in an audit trail when an agent needs to call Salesforce, provision a resource, or hand off to a sub-agent. The sandbox piece identified this layer as being absent. The database component argued for is the blast radius control, which is applicable to all corporate APIs. The same architectural pattern—short-lived, narrowly scoped, auditable proxy credentials with policy decisions kept apart from credential delivery—is described in the IETF draft.

Behavioral telemetry with identity awareness. The LLM evaluation element sought observability that was rooted in identity and extracted from the model layer. Not only did the model make a mistake, but we also need to know who approved what, whether the result complied with the policy that approved it, and whether we can convince an auditor.

5.6 The Future of Responsible and Sustainable AI

The issue of designing AI that is simultaneously realistic and ethical is one of the top priorities of the day. In connection with the integration of AI technology into our lives, it is crucial to ensure that this technology is both ethical, transparent, and sustainable over time. This is true for all areas of activity, from medicine and education to finance and government, as well as ecology. Sustainable and responsible AI requires an interdisciplinary approach involving various aspects such as ethics, environment, and governance, to name a few.

Responsible AI can therefore be understood as being based on the principles of ethical, fair, and accountable AI development and deployment processes. Some of the ideas promoted in responsible AI include nondiscrimination, transparency, privacy, and explainability. But sustainable AI extends this concept even further by incorporating economic, social, and environmental sustainability into the entire lifespan of the AI. The combination of all of these ideas ensures that the impact of AI is not only positive but sustainable for both humans and the environment.

Responsibility in AI for the future should entail greater attention towards ethics in the development process of AI. Ethics should be considered at every stage in the life cycle of AI – from the acquisition of data and training of models, through to deployment and monitoring – as an increasing number of companies are starting to realize. This includes ensuring that AI technologies do not exacerbate existing inequalities and addressing concerns such as algorithmic bias, whereby some parties unfairly receive different outcomes. Human supervision within ethical AI design is critical for the same reason.

The ability to explain and explain AI decisions is yet another critical breakthrough that will have an impact on AI in the future. As AI decisions made by advanced AI models become harder to interpret, the researchers working on explainable AI (XAI) are trying to find ways to make decisions transparent to the individuals affected by them. Transparency is essential for stakeholders to evaluate the validity and impartiality of AI systems, thus playing a vital role in making them popular.

In ensuring the future development of responsible AI, regulation and governance shall be highly important. In making sure that AI systems are utilized in an ethical manner and safely, regulatory systems are developed by both governments and international bodies. In essence, these regulatory systems have the objective of laying out principles to manage risks, act responsibly, and protect information. By way of example, AI systems that fall into the high-risk category are regulated even more strictly via risk-based regulatory systems, where AI systems are classified depending on their potential effects. To make sure that they continue to comply with the law as regulations evolve, companies should ensure compliance.

In relation to the organizational environment, the role of governance models for AI is bound to become increasingly relevant. The governance framework provides some structured ways of handling any risks associated with AI and having a sense of responsibility regarding the development of AI. The guidelines, processes, and other forms of management are aimed at governing the development and use of the AI. It is very important to have audits, governance boards, and ethics committees monitoring the activities of the AI.

The persistence of the technology over a long period of time is another key issue that needs to be considered. It should be noted that there is skepticism about the long-run sustainability of AI technology, owing to its negative impact on the environment, especially the amount of energy consumed during the training of large models. As a result, "green AI" has become increasingly popular in recent times – the development of AI technology that has minimal effect on the environment. This entails the use of renewable sources of energy, developing energy-efficient hardware, and algorithm optimization.

Social sustainability is equally as significant as environmental sustainability when making choices. Rather than designing technologies that cater to a select group of elites, artificial intelligence technology needs to be developed in a way that benefits the greater human population as a whole. The effects that automation will have on the workforce, opening up participation in online communities for more individuals, and ensuring that everyone has equal access to artificial intelligence technology is all encompassed within this idea.

Advances in human-AI interaction technology will also shape the future development path of responsible AI. There is a growing trend towards using artificial intelligence to improve the capabilities of humans, rather than replace the decision-making process performed by humans. This results in better decisions being made, as well as more information being available through the cooperation between humans and technology. For example, in the medical field, AI can help doctors make diagnoses; however, the decision-making process remains in the hands of the doctors themselves.

Responsibility of data privacy and data governance will continue to be integral in artificial intelligence ethics. The smooth functioning of artificial intelligence technology requires ensuring that the data remains secure and private. Data governance issues, including data protection, data ownership, and consent, are some of the areas that have to be addressed. The use of privacy-preserving methods through federated learning and differential privacy enables data access for research purposes while safeguarding individual privacy rights.

Another trend in the making involves the use of artificial intelligence methods where there is accountability and auditing. Due to having been put through rigorous testing by third parties, the artificial intelligence process will reveal any form of biases, risks, and mistakes that may have been made. The operators of the artificial intelligence process should not be concerned since audits will ensure that the system performs well. There will be enough reason to blame the company if the artificial intelligence process does anything wrong.

There is a possibility that one might have hope for the future with the integration of artificial intelligence into sustainability projects across the globe. Problems like climate change, provision of health services, and food safety, among others, are some of the problems experienced across the world, but then again, there can be solutions for these problems through AI technology.

Creating sustainable and ethical AI systems, however, does come with its share of problems. First, one of the main issues faced involves the absence of any standard in AI ethics and governance. There might be a variance in approach adopted by nations and organizations, because of which it becomes essential to come up with a global agreement on AI standards. Another problem related to the fact that technology changes much faster than regulatory and governance structures are capable of keeping up is present as well. The more technologies in the area of AI develop and evolve, the more important it becomes for organizations and policymakers to adapt constantly. Efficient regulation should be based on anticipation as well as continuous observation and improvement.

However, the problem of trust is also equally important here. The amount of trust that an individual would have with regards to an AI system is based on how reliable, impartial, and transparent the system is. In case of failure in the AI system, trust is bound to be lost. The creation of ethical artificial intelligence is highly dependent upon whether or not we can successfully raise awareness among the general population. Both the people and organizations would need to be aware of the capabilities and risks associated with artificial intelligence. We need to increase our understanding of the technology among citizens, governments, and software engineers.

Thus, one can define the concept of responsible and sustainable AI as a period of innovation and discovery that coexist in accordance with moral values and responsibility. The mission for businesses would be to make use of AI to the fullest extent while inflicting no harm whatsoever.

Multiple Choice Questions (MCQs)

1. **What is the primary purpose of an AI governance framework?**
   A. To increase computational speed
   B. To ensure ethical, compliant, and responsible AI use
   C. To replace human decision-making
   D. To reduce data storage costs
2. **Which of the following is a key component of an AI governance framework?**
   A. Random data generation
   B. Clear policies and accountability structures
   C. Unlimited automation
   D. Ignoring regulatory requirements
3. **What role do AI governance committees primarily play?**
   A. Writing code for AI systems
   B. Overseeing ethical and regulatory compliance
   C. Managing hardware infrastructure
   D. Marketing AI products
4. **Which organizational role is typically responsible for ensuring AI compliance?**
   A. Graphic Designer
   B. Data Governance Officer
   C. Sales Executive
   D. Network Technician

5. **Why is continuous monitoring important in AI systems?**

   A. To reduce electricity consumption

   B. To identify performance issues and biases over time

   C. To eliminate the need for training data

   D. To automate all decisions permanently

6. **Which method helps improve AI systems over time?**

   A. Ignoring feedback

   B. Periodic audits and performance evaluation

   C. Removing governance policies

   D. Limiting data access completely

7. **What is the goal of an AI incident management plan?**

   A. To prevent all AI development

   B. To respond effectively to failures or ethical breaches

   C. To increase system complexity

   D. To reduce employee involvement

8. **Which of the following is an example of an AI incident?**

   A. Faster processing speed

   B. Biased decision-making output

   C. Improved accuracy

   D. Reduced training time

9. **What is a key focus of sustainable AI development?**
   A. Maximizing profits only
   B. Minimizing environmental and societal impact
   C. Ignoring long-term effects
   D. Eliminating governance structures
10. **The future of AI governance is expected to emphasize:**
   A. Complete automation without oversight
   B. Stronger regulations and human-AI collaboration
   C. Elimination of ethics in AI
   D. Reduced transparency

Answers

1	2	3	4	5	6	7	8	9	10
B	B	B	B	B	B	B	B	B	B

Bibliography

Agarwal, P. (2024). *AI Ethics and Legal Compliance Dr. Pooja Agarwal.* Ink of Knowledge.

Ai2i. (2025). 9 Key AI Governance Frameworks in 2025.

Calvert, T. (2020). *Regulation, Compliance and Ethics in Law Firms.* Globe Law & Business.

Carlton, D. (2024). *AI Governance: Applying AI Policy and Ethics through Principles and Assessments.* Technics Publications.

Debique, K. (2026). The agent stack is missing two layers and the field just figured it out. *Www.Oleria.Com.* Retrieved from https://www.oleria.com/blog/the-agent-stack-is-missing-two-layers

Fitz-Gerald, A., Ganesh, V., Nathwani, J., Niazi, M., & Herdem, M. S. (2026). *Foundational Principles of AI Governance and Policy. Frontiers of Artificial Intelligence, Ethics and Multidisciplinary Applications.* Cham: Springer Nature Switzerland.

Fregly, C. (2025). *Ai Systems Performance Engineering: Optimizing Model Training and Inference Workloads With Gpus, Cuda, and Pytorch.* Oreilly & Associates Inc.

Geeksforgeeks. (2026). Explainable Artificial Intelligence(XAI).

Hendricks, A. (2024). How Do I Identify Key Stakeholders?

Infotech, C. (2023). 9 Ethical AI Principles For Organizations To Follow.

JSA. (2024). Privacy And Data Protection In Artificial Intelligence.

Lu, Q., Zhu, L., Whittle, J., & Xu, X. (2023). *Responsible AI: Best Practices for Creating Trustworthy AI Systems*. Addison-Wesley Professional.

Marwala, T. (2024). Framework for the Governance of Artificial Intelligence.

Meyes, R. (2022). *Transparency and Interpretability for Learned Representations of Artificial Neural Networks*. Springer Vieweg.

Rafter, M. (2025). What Is Risk Assessment And Mitigation? Meaning, Advantages, Framework, Types and Tools & Techniques Used. *Eventussecurity*.

Tarud, J. (2025). Bias and Fairness in AI: Understanding the Challenges and Solutions.

Taylor, J. E. (2025). *AI Governance & Strategy: The Blueprint for Scale, Sustainability, and Impact in Healthcare AI Transformation (AI in Healthcare Leadership Series Book 2)*. Pages By The Lake, LLC.

Team, L. (2024). AI Governance.

About The Author

Dinesh Rajasekharan is a seasoned product and technology leader with over a decade of experience building secure, scalable solutions across cloud and enterprise environments. He has led high-impact initiatives in security, identity, access management, privacy, and platform development at global organizations such as Amazon, Salesforce, Oracle, and Symend. His expertise spans authentication, authorization, API security, compliance, data protection, and developer platforms.

Throughout his career, Dinesh has focused on enabling organizations to innovate while embedding trust, governance, and security into their systems by design. He brings a strong blend of business strategy and technical insight, working at the intersection of architecture and responsible technology adoption. An inventor with patents in authorization and API technologies, he is also deeply interested in the evolving governance of AI and digital platforms. He holds executive education from Kellogg School of Management and a degree in Computer Science from Vellore Institute of Technology.Lorerat re la diatibu stistiat.

Apic tem et hillabo reserio quam, offictatur aligendipsus repel eicabo. Uptaspi derchillor aut faccupta venimusam sa doluptur, sunt aut exere cone la dolut as et fugiam aut fuga. Ut dis rem et laut aperrovitas et quis etus illaborrunt.

Us et es magnisciam fugias ut ipiet expla nonessum ad molora adipsunti omnimpore, se ium ni at.

Aquam, consequas arum fugit accum repernatur, ullia qui dolor res eum arupta vel is magnimus auta nam eum et et magnihi cillorehenti quatem inullut et autatiur reiciminum volorpo rehendame nust utem ab ius nos magnis et od mos ut veles deliqui de verum dellit, ellab ipicili taeperrum et laborrumque pedionsedis expel expliqu aeptatiist, quo omnisciae. Et explit ent, consequi optas a quunda non recto et eum verroru mquaepresed qui nos es eum int, que optur, nos volupti busamen duntotam comnimo lorerro exercim agnisinto officil loreste mquatios aut que consed ut volupis cust enectus danihicid maio consed mos et litem. Ut quunt omnim fuga. Ullorit, sin ratur maio volum ipsa et et, officae vit, et aut dolor molorerum velignam, cum laborep udipis rempori volupta sitasit aepeliquias eicias porae moloria cuptate odiassum nisitio nsedipi deligen delique omnime vollatur, quidel im iliquae. Sed et mod mint quatiis andia natis earum alia sum, sequi to beria quatet ipid exernam eaque vero ipsamet lacid moluptatae esequas sitatur reicae et odi aut qui doluptatquo oditatur molorro volut into qui beatatur re nonseque nonectat.

Equatin ullaccus dolum harit experru ntibeaqui tem nonsequate et haribea serumquunt et harum fugiaer ibustem sa eserovit, in porem dignimaio veliquis mo odit, nimoluptate eatiunt alibus aboratia nimus vel estium et endem acea dolorit id ut volora dolenit as dolores eum eni ut vendestiumet omniate nducias itaspernam, ut restius antus, optat quod quis il et, utate sinciat ecatior ibustrum expelest pliate exerume maximendest volorest, nobitatas sum facepe voluptur?

Pa cus elit idis delenis ende velitat et aligent landanditat.

Onem dolorio nseque porat est, sit es imendam arum volupta tempersperi restiossi del ma cus minctae cuptiorio commodipsam, commo min et faciet qui de consequi dolorum, sum eum dolupta cus rae voluptamus volorer erciat et hitataspel estiisto que senda versped molendunt elitata que nonem re ditis audia qui odisitem si ium vel mo ex ero bla simpore

www.ingramcontent.com/pod-product-compliance
Lightning Source LLC
LaVergne TN
LVHW022205200926
848481LV00006B/1858
* 9 7 9 8 9 0 5 1 0 4 8 0 0 *